# Miracle in the Hills

*by* MARY T. MARTIN SLOOP, M.D.
*with* LEGETTE BLYTHE

McGRAW-HILL BOOK COMPANY, INC.

*New York*    *Toronto*    *London*

MIRACLE IN THE HILLS

Published by the McGraw-Hill Book Company, Inc.

PRINTED IN THE UNITED STATES OF AMERICA

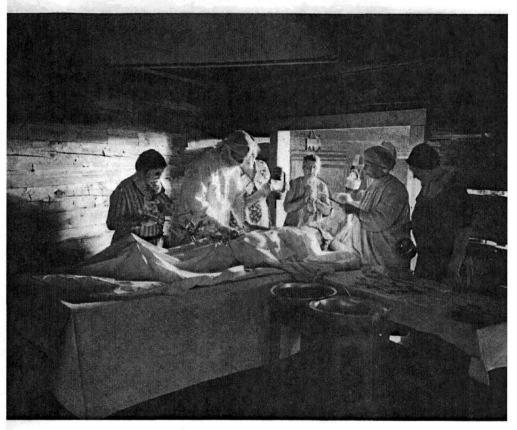

The two Doctors Sloop—Eustace (left) and the author—performing an operation in a mountain cabin about 1917.

*To my husband,*
*the Doctor*

# List of Illustrations

# Foreword

IN my career as a newspaperman, I have interviewed countless persons—presidents, panhandlers, pickpockets and princes, bishops and burglars, explorers and opera singers and yoyo champions—the great and the lowly, the good and the bad and the in-betweens. But never have I encountered a character more truly unique than Dr. Mary T. Martin Sloop. No mold shaped her, no die stamped her out.

Until this book brought us together, I had never met her, although all my life I had heard of Crossnore's two Doctors Sloop and their extraordinary accomplishments. I shall never forget that first visit to Crossnore. I reached the Sloop home at eight-thirty one Friday night, expecting to meet a quiet and perhaps even doddering old lady of almost eighty. Instead a vivacious, smiling, chattering little person met me at the door. She wore rimless glasses and behind them her eyes fairly sparkled. Her hair was white, her mouth wide and generous. There was about her an air of unquenchable energy, a contagious vitality. That night she told stories steadily and entertainingly until eleven. The next morning at eight she was at her school office. All day she attended to countless administrative tasks; that evening she made a speech at a dinner of returning business-class graduates; and afterward she square danced until eleven. This was my doddering old pioneer doctor and educator!

Dr. Sloop always refers to her husband, Dr. Eustace Sloop, as simply "Doctor." He is a tall, exceedingly handsome man with a fine head of white hair, a white mustache, and a clipped white beard. Doctor carries on his medical practice as strenuously today as he did some forty years ago. Her story and his are inseparable; everything they did for Crossnore and the mountain people they did together.

The techniques used in getting Dr. Sloop's story varied. Sometimes she talked into a tape recorder, at other times I took copious notes. I have been to Crossnore countless times, but my interviews with Dr. Sloop have always been more pleasure than work. I have tried hard to preserve her own words, expressions, and tone. These are her stories, and this is the way she tells them.

Dr. Sloop's work has attracted national attention. She has received special citations and honorary degrees. In 1951 she was named American Mother of the Year. But I do not like to think of her as a special or extraordinary person. She is, rather, one of our last examples of the sturdy, energetic pioneer woman who played such an important role in the settling of America. She is a woman of tremendous faith, both in God and in herself. This combination has proved more than a match for ignorance, poverty, and sickness in the mountains.

But already I embarrass her with fancy words. She is no fancy woman. She is solid, as solid and true as the great mountain people of whom she speaks with such warmth and affection. Nor did she and the Doctor do their great work out of any grim sense of duty. They did it joyously, exuberantly, with a gleam—and often a wink—in their eyes.

It has been a rewarding experience working with her. What is more, it has been great fun.

*LeGette Blythe*

*Huntersville, N.C.*

# 1

FROM my office in the center of the Administration Building here at Crossnore School I can see outside in two directions. I can look down or up, I can recall past days of struggle and challenge and modest achievement, or I can foresee in imagination larger challenges and greater accomplishments in the years ahead.

Through the window at my right I can look down the hill, a long way down toward the little circle of level land that is the heart of the village of Crossnore. It was here in the long ago that old George Crossnore kept store and here some years later stood the old shed that was the first school building in this community.

But if I turn my head slightly to the left and look out through the short hallway and the front door, I can see up the steep slope, past the music building and the dining hall and the Middle Girls' dormitory and even beyond the bell tower toward the gymnasium and the new Big Boys' dormitory on the other side of the athletic field.

Through the window I can see all the way down the hill, except where trees and rhododendrons and mountain laurels screen off the view, to the place where that old school building crouched in the flat. I can see—and well I can remember —the very birth spot of Crossnore School as it looked more than twoscore years ago.

But looking toward the left, I cannot see to the top of the slope and the end of the Crossnore campus on that side; the rectangle of the open doorway provides only a limited view. Nor can I see—but I am thankful that I am privileged still to dream—how high and how far Crossnore in the days to come will climb.

The Administration Building sits only a little above the point from which we began to grow upward, and yet in that day when we built it we felt that we were far up the hill and along the rising path. I sit here in my office from day to day, and nearing eighty years of age I look down the hill and back through many years. But I am thankful to a kind Providence that I can still look also—and more often do—out through the door that frames a view up the hill.

It's interesting how towns get their names, don't you think?

It was about the middle of the last century, the old folks around here say, that George Crossnore moved into the community and bought land on which he planned to raise cattle. On this little spot which is now the center of Crossnore, the only level area of any size hereabouts, he built a one-room store with a little lean-to in the back for his living quarters. He was never married, as far as people in this section knew. Soon George Crossnore became the leading citizen in the sparsely settled region.

Twelve miles north, almost on the Tennessee line, were the iron mines, operated by a New Jersey company. The quality of the ore was excellent, and the pig iron smelted down by charcoal made at Cranberry Gap—called that because of the immense cranberry bogs there—was hauled out over a little narrow-gauge railroad. In the course of time the Southern Railway extended its line from Salisbury in the direction of Asheville as far as Morganton. The old people say that the beginning of the Civil War caused work on that road to stop when it reached Morganton. At any rate, there was no railroad between Cranberry and Morganton, and so the mail was carried by an old man who traveled that route. And the route brought him by George Crossnore's store.

There were hardly any roads in those days—only trails that led along creek bottoms and often in the beds of the streams.

When the weather was good, this old man, the story is, would ride his beast, but when it was foul he went afoot. As all mountain people will understand, that was because he did not dare run the risk of having his horse break a leg in fording some rocky, swiftly flowing stream.

The mailman would always stop at George Crossnore's store to warm himself at the potbellied stove in the wintertime, and to exchange the news with the storekeeper.

In those days there was a woman living in the community who was something of a rarity. She was determined to keep up with what was going on in the world, so she took a weekly newspaper. But it was a long trip each week to Cranberry to get that paper, so she appealed to George Crossnore to have a post office established in the community.

One day she was at the store when the old mailman stopped.

"Here's your man," Mr. Crossnore said to her, as he pointed to the mail carrier. "He's the fellow to see about gettin' a post office."

So they talked about the problem. The mailman thought it might be arranged, and he asked what she thought the post office should be named if the Post Office Department agreed to establish it there.

"I don't care what the name is just so long as I can get my paper and keep me and my young 'uns posted on what's agoin' on in the world," she told him.

"Well, I'll see what can be done about it," he said. "And if they give you 'uns a post office, I want 'em to name it for the kindest-hearted man I ever knew, and that's George Crossnore."

The post office was established in George Crossnore's store, and it was named Crossnore. To this day in Crossnore, North Carolina, I understand, is the only post office by that name in the United States.

Little else has been recorded of George Crossnore. After

living some fifty years in this community, he moved away. Years ago I asked Uncle Newt Clark—he wasn't my uncle; we call many old men in the mountains "Uncle" simply as a term of affectionate respect—I asked him where Mr. Crossnore came from. Uncle Newt was one of our best local historians.

When I asked him that question, he seemed puzzled.

"Well," he drawled, after a while, "I jes' never thought to aks him."

"When he left here, then, Uncle Newt," I said, "where'd he go?"

Again his face was thoughtful. "I knowed him a many a year," he said, "and I was at the store the day he closed up and pulled out. But I jes' never thought to aks George Crossnore where he was agoin'."

The little store of the old bachelor has long ago vanished. So has the first school building. I am sorry, especially that the school has disappeared. They tore it down years ago when I was away on a trip. I'd like to have it standing down there in the flat. I could show it to our visitors and then lead them up the slope to our fine new consolidated high-school building and the dormitories and all the rest. They could see then how far Crossnore has advanced in forty years. We have come a long way—from that old boarded-up shed in the flat to our twenty-five buildings clutching the steep side of the long hill. But maybe it's best that the old school's gone. Maybe I brag too much as it is.

2

I HAVE always loved the mountains. As a child going with my family to the mountains in the summer I was always thrilled when we began to get up into the high hills. Because I have lived in them more than half my life and have come to know the mountain people so well, I suppose the mountains have got into my blood.

Frequently someone from the lower country says to me, "Mrs. Sloop, I just can't stay in the mountains more than a few days at a time. I love the scenery; I think the mountains are beautiful. But after a day or two they begin to crowd down upon me and choke me. I can't see out. I feel as though I were about to suffocate. If I could just get on top and see beyond them, maybe it would be different. But it seems that there is always a huge mountain cutting off my vision. I seem always to be in a valley, hemmed in from the rest of the world, imprisoned."

I can understand that feeling. I was born and reared in the Piedmont region of North Carolina, the great and beautiful rolling land between the mountains and the coastal plain. In the mountains you never see out all around you, of course. But I don't have the feeling of being fenced in. Instead, I feel on top of the world, even though I may be in a sheltered little valley. To me the mountains are inspiring, uplifting, challenging. They seem to beckon to higher things.

Have you ever observed how a mountain man or woman who lives down in the lower country must get back now and then—as often as he can manage it—to the mountains? Give him a day or two away from his work, and he'll go flying back to the mountains like a homing pigeon. You can get a mountain man out of the mountains, as the old saying goes, but you can't get the mountains out of the mountain men.

This is a characteristic of mountain people in all lands, no doubt. I know it's true of our people of the southern Appalachians. The Appalachians, the geologists say, are very old mountains. Some declare they are the oldest in the world, though how they can figure it I cannot understand. Back in the days of Dr. Elisha Mitchell, who measured the towering peak that now bears his name, I understand they said that our Appalachians were millions of years old. But I had no idea they were as old as some of the scientists today say they are. In fact, I had no idea the world was that old.

Some time ago I was reading about a report that a Yale professor of geology had made at a meeting of the American Association for the Advancement of Science. This gentleman was telling about the age of the Appalachians. He said that the first great Appalachian range arose some 800 million years ago, very likely before there was any life on this planet. Over many millions of years, he said, these great mountains, once probably higher than Mount Everest's 29,000 feet, were worn down until finally they were washed into the ocean.

Then, said this professor, about 600 million years ago a second range of Appalachians was thrust up, and after another 200 million or so this range in turn washed down. Some 350 million years ago the third range arose. By this time the land was covered with vegetation: that was the beginning of the period when the coal deposits were being laid down. In these great forests of tree ferns lived the most primitive of the backboned animals.

But this range lasted only 100 million years, and our present one was raised much higher some 50 million years later by great earth convulsions. It is steadily wearing away, but our Yale man assures us that it will be here many millions of years before it in turn washes into the sea.

How did he find out all this history of our Appalachians? He determined the ages of various Appalachian rocks from the rate of decay of radioactive minerals, such as uranium and thorium. Fragments of these various ranges remain, and their ages can be measured. It is truly amazing what these scientists in this atomic age are doing. Just reading about it leaves an old-time country doctor wide-eyed with wonder.

From the ridge out in front of my house at Crossnore I can look across other ridges and over there in the northwest see Grandfather Mountain. Often a filmy white cloud ob-

6

scures him; but when the cloud moves on, there he is, lying flat upon his back looking into the sky, his nose, his chin, his beard, his chest, his hands folded at his waist, his long legs outlined clearly against the blue beyond.

Grandfather, some geologists believe, is the oldest rock on the face of the earth. I wonder. I have walked many times over him, I have raced past him along the beautiful Blue Ridge Parkway. Yet I never go near him or even look out upon him from the ridge above my home without experiencing a feeling of awe. Can it be that I am looking upon the oldest bit of the Creator's handiwork upon the surface of His earth?

My old bones may be aching, for I'm an ancient rock myself—though I insist I'm no fossil. But even eighty years, by some standards of measurement, is a mighty short period. And when I look upon Grandfather I feel young, and transient. And very humble.

# 3

MY home is in the mountains and has been for almost half a century. My children are here, and my grandchildren, and many, many beloved friends. I call myself a mountain woman, and I plan to live out my remaining days here at Crossnore.

But I'm an outlander, a come-lately. Many mountain families trace their lines, unbroken, back beyond the Revolutionary War, and not a generation in those long years has forsaken the hill country. Yet not even my parents were mountain people.

Father was from Richmond, Virginia, and Mother was reared in the low country, at Wilmington, North Carolina. Both cities were far from the mountains, and even farther in customs and traditions.

Part of me—of every man and woman, in fact—is my

parents and the lives they led. And, in my case, I suspect, their war. Yet, though I am proud of the lives and feats of my Southern ancestors, I have never been one to keep fighting the War Between the States. I have little patience with those *professional* Confederates who, from the safe retreats of musty library reference rooms and armed with genealogical charts, wage relentlessly their wars of resounding words.

Father was a graduate of the University of Virginia. He was teaching in Washington and Jefferson College in western Pennsylvania when Dr. Elisha Mitchell, an eminent professor at the University of North Carolina, lost his life on the towering mountain, the highest in eastern America, they later named for him. Dr. Mitchell died on June 27, 1857. Shortly afterward Father was called to Chapel Hill to take Dr. Mitchell's chair.

When the Civil War came on, Father was chosen by the students and the younger professors to form a military company and drill it.

"Where did you ever learn military tactics?" I asked him years later. "You never did go to military school, did you?"

"I studied them at night," he replied, "and taught them in the daytime."

Father went out as captain of that Chapel Hill company, and came back a colonel, after four years of fighting and three times being wounded. It was during this tragic period that he met Mother. Early in the war he had been sent down to Fort Caswell in the extreme southeastern tip of the state below Wilmington. One of his friends was a young man named Jack Costin, who lived at Wilmington. One day he asked Captain Martin to go home with him for the week end.

Father went, and that night the two attended a dance for the soldiers. There he met one of Jack Costin's sisters. He danced with her. When the waltz came on, they started to waltz. But Jack came up and said, "Remember, 'Titia, Father doesn't allow you girls to waltz with gentlemen."

8

So they had to wait for the square dance before they could begin dancing again. Despite this obstacle, that was the night he fell in love with Letitia Coddington Costin, my mother. Soon they were married.

For a while Father's company remained in the vicinity of Wilmington. But then came orders to move. So Father took Mother up to Fifth Creek in Iredell County, where one of her sisters, married to a minister who had become a chaplain in the Confederate Army, was living.

Some of the old slaves had refused to be freed in accordance with President Lincoln's proclamation and had chosen to stay there to take care of their beloved Mis' Nolie, as they called Mother's sister. Her name was Naomi, but everybody called her Nolie. I never knew why.

So the two sisters stayed there in the care of the old Negroes, who vowed to protect them in case any soldiers came by. And soldiers came. I'll never forget Mother's story about the time that Stoneman's Raiders galloped up. It made a vivid impression upon my youthful mind.

They had heard from a man hurrying ahead on horseback that the dreaded raiders were on their way. These were the men who had left Georgia in such condition that it was said a crow could not live over the route along which they had passed.

Soon they did come—right into the house where Aunt Nolie and Mother were. The faithful Negroes stayed with them. But little was left for the raiders to get, especially food, and they began to fuss because they couldn't find anything to eat.

"We ain't got nothin' t'eat but some apple butter," one of the old Negro women said to a soldier. "Do you like apple butter?"

"Yes," one soldier replied. "I come from New England, and that's where the apple butter is best."

"Well," she said, "there's some in that crock. You can have

9

some if you want to." And she handed him a big spoon.

He dipped the spoon full, opened his mouth wide, and took it all in.

The apple butter had been a failure. It had burned, and it was the bitterest thing on the face of the earth. And the old darky stood and laughed while the marauding fellow spit and spit and spit, trying to get rid of it.

But another story she told of that same visit by Stoneman's Raiders always made my blood boil. And it still does!

There was a long trunk there that Grandfather had given Mother when she was a girl, as a birthday gift. She was very proud of it, because it was long enough to take her skirts without folding them, so there'd be no wrinkles. One of the soldiers kicked it. "That's got ammunition in it," he said. "That ain't no trunk. It's just got ammunition in it. Open it up!"

So they took a hammer and broke the lock and opened it.

On the tiptop was Mother's prized bonnet. It was a little poke bonnet covered with feathers of tropical birds, which a sea captain had brought her. This sea captain came often, and the girls were very fond of him. Their father—my grandfather—was a commission merchant in Wilmington. Whenever the captains came into port on their fruit ships, he thought it was inhospitable to let them go to one of the hotels, which were none too good at that time. So he always invited them to stay in his home.

This captain would always bring presents to the five girls in the family. This lovely little bonnet had been one of his presents to Mother.

The soldier picked up the bonnet, looked at it. The others laughed at him because that was the ammunition he had said they would find in the trunk. They asked him what kind of gun that was.

He threw it down, he was so mad, and with his muddy boots ground that little bonnet to shreds.

Mother could hardly hold her tongue. But the old darky

10

kept whispering, "Don't you sass him, Mis' 'Titia, don't you sass him. He might git mad and do worse!"

She used to talk a lot about that little feathered bonnet, and how she did wish we still had it; she'd like so much to see her daughters wear that bonnet.

There's still another story of my family and their war that through the years has persisted in my memory. The war had come to an end. Mother was still up at Fifth Creek with Mis' Nolie and had not seen Father for a long while. Soldiers began coming home, the exhausted Confederates, trudging slowly and wearily and often in pain. They stopped at homes along the route and were given rest and food—if there was any food—and care if they were sick. All the homes were open to them, though the people had so little to offer. That had been the case at Aunt Nolie's home, and they were used to it.

Then one day they looked out and saw a pitiful-looking gray horse coming slowly up the road, and in the saddle was a man reeling from side to side as he clutched the pommel.

"There comes a poor drunk soldier," they said.

Aunt Nolie's husband, the chaplain, had gotten home a day or two earlier. They called him and told him that the soldier coming down the road was drunk. He went out to receive the man, and when the old horse stopped, told him to lean over and fall on his shoulder.

The women helped him carry the soldier in and lay him on the porch. He lay there a little while. He had a beard, and the dust of the road covered his sweat-streaked face. One of them bathed his face with some cool water to try to make him feel better. But he didn't show any interest in anything. Then after some moments he opened his eyes and looked straight into the eyes of the chaplain.

"Why, Brother William," the chaplain exclaimed, "we didn't know it was you!"

Then they took my father into the house and gave him a hot bath. But he was too weak to sit up. As he lay on the bed he told of the great kindness he had experienced along the road, when people gave him bits of food—food he had shared with his old horse, and Father's horse had been such a beautiful animal!—and the great effort he had made to get back to his folks.

And that's how my father, a colonel in the Confederate Army, came home from the war.

Years later Father used to tell us children how he had insisted on sharing his food with his horse. If he hadn't done so, he declared, the horse would have died. All through that ravaged country there wasn't anything left even for a horse to eat.

4

FATHER returned to the university after the war; but the poverty of those terrible times soon closed its doors, and he obtained a teaching position in a small military school near Nashville, Tennessee.

From there he was shortly called to Davidson College, a little Presbyterian institution some thirty years old, in the west-central section of North Carolina. They wanted him to teach geology and chemistry and serve also as bursar, and they told him he was greatly needed. He accepted and came to Davidson.

He and Mother were now a hundred miles west of Chapel Hill and two hundred from Wilmington and the coast, but they were still a hundred miles from the foothills of the Blue Ridge when I arrived in the family.

I was born in Davidson, just across the street from the president's house, into which we moved when I was three months old. All my young days were lived there. That old house, in which the present president of Davidson College, Dr. John R. Cunningham, and his family live, is the house in which

Mrs. Stonewall Jackson was born when her father, Dr. Morrison, was president of Davidson. As you go into the front door, the room in which she was born is on the left side of the hallway. Don't forget to look in.

Father and Mother had ten children, but only two of us are living today. The other is Mrs. Archibald Currie of Davidson, who lives just up the street from the house in which I was born.

My schooling before Father sent me off to college had been gained in a little one-teacher school at Davidson, which I attended until I was fifteen. When I was ready to go away to school, my parents differed over where I should be sent. Mother, having been reared in Wilmington and being the daughter of a family very fond of social life, felt that girls should be educated only in finishing schools. Father, on the other hand, admired the education of Dr. Mitchell's two sisters, who read their Bible in Greek and did other things comparable.

So he decided to send me to a college where I might get an education in more than charming manners, and he announced that I was going to college in Statesville, twenty miles north of Davidson.

I protested. Not because I didn't like the school (I knew hardly anything about it), but because of its name. I simply couldn't stand the name, Statesville Female College, and in order that even the wayfaring stranger though he be a fool might know who was entrusted to its tender care—for Women. Statesville Female College for Women, indeed! They long ago changed its name—to Mitchell College—and I am glad, for I still think "female" one of the most horrible words in the English language.

I didn't want to go to that college, too, I suspect, because I had grown up on the edge of the campus where the boys lived, and I liked boys. Now, at the age of eighty, it's safe for me to admit it. But Father thought that it was the best college from an academic point of view available to me, for we hadn't the money for me to go to an expensive one.

In 1891 I was graduated from that institution, and went home to find Mother practically an invalid. I stayed for years in Davidson to nurse her. In that time I took some studies in Davidson College, choosing those that were pre-med, though I never told Mother that I intended to be a medical missionary.

Nor did Father know that in my childhood I had been impressed particularly by two guests whom we had entertained in our home, Dr. and Mrs. McGilvary, missionaries to Siam from the Northern Presbyterian Church. I became very devoted to them and admired their work and the way in which they had endured times of persecution and trouble and uncertainty in that foreign country.

The McGilvarys talked particularly about the difficulty of getting medical service and how so many people died whose lives could have been saved if only the missionaries had been doctors.

Although I was only about five years old then, I can remember going off by myself after hearing them talk on one occasion and promising the Lord that when I grew up I was going to be a medical missionary to Siam. That is when I first got the idea of being a doctor.

As I grew a little older, I became interested also in teaching the little darkies around us. I began with the children of our cook, who lived in a house out in the back yard. Every Sunday afternoon she dressed them up, fixed their hair—I particularly admired the way she platted it—and sent them up to the back porch of our home for their Sunday-school lesson.

Those little pickaninnies' names intrigue me to this day. The oldest was a boy, and I well remember *his* name: it was Ptolemy Philadelphus White. And he certainly wasn't white. His education began right then and continued until he became the first registered pharmacist of the colored race in South Carolina. His mother couldn't read or write.

The oldest little girl's name was Hannah Chaney Isabella Ukezene White. The next one was Liza Charleston Bassey Narcissus White. I don't remember the names of the younger ones; I don't think they were peculiar. But I was stumped each time the mother came to me and asked me to write down these names for christening (for she saw to it that each one was christened). And as they grew older and began to study the Presbyterian catechism, I remained interested in them, and no one was happier than I at the later success of Ptolemy Philadelphus. He was the most distinguished alumnus of my first class.

Speaking of those long names reminds me: we can cap Liza's name with that of one of Dr. Sloop's patients, also a Negro. I couldn't vouch for this, but they do say that his name is on record at the courthouse. It went this way, and I hope I'm not leaving out any part of it: George Washington Christopher Columbus Come Here Cellar Door Kings Mountain While Them Hounds Run That Fox Listen To The Heavenly Music Hemphill Catfish Jackson.

As time went on I became a teacher in an organized Negro Sunday school at Davidson. I learned that our denomination, the Southern Presbyterian, had no missionaries in Siam. But since I had become so interested in the work among the Negroes, I thought that I had better volunteer for assignment as a missionary to Africa. I was then still only a child.

So when at thirteen years of age I joined the church and old Dr. Rumple in talking with me privately asked what kind of church work I thought I would do as I grew older, I told him not to tell Father and Mother but that I had become interested in being a foreign missionary. I had promised to be one, I assured him, and a medical missionary, at that. He said, "What'll your mother say about your studying medicine?"

"I believe it'd kill her," I told him. "So I'm not going to tell her." I wasn't old enough to face the problem.

Nor did I ever change my mind about studying medicine.

So I went off to Statesville Female College for Women, and at eighteen I was graduated; and I expected to go right on with my education.

But Mother's illness for twelve years gave me all I could do at home; though I did continue my studies at Davidson College, a part of the time as that school's only coed. At first Mother insisted that I take my lessons in Father's study where she could be the chaperone for the professor and me. Fortunately that professor was a married man and middle-aged, so she didn't have to come in very often.

But she did not like the subjects I chose. I had to compromise for a while by taking French, which was a ladylike subject, in order to get the science and math that I wanted. When I suggested that I'd like to take junior math, which included surveying, she nearly fainted, and she flatly refused to allow me to do it. Such a thing was most unladylike, even though I promised to study French at the same time. I could *not* take math and I could *not* take surveying, and that was that! Later, when I came to the mountains, I needed so very much to know how to help my husband who was the only surveyor in our community at that time.

After Mother's death I prepared to go to medical school. The first year's work I took at Davidson. In those days the North Carolina Medical College had the first two years at Davidson and the last two in Charlotte.

But at Davidson they would not let me study anatomy, so the next year, I knew, I would have to go to a woman's medical college. It wasn't considered proper at all for me to go into a dissecting room with all those naked cadavers lying about on the dissecting tables! That indeed would have been highly unladylike. The neighbors would never have recovered from the shock of hearing about it.

# 5

IN my medical class I quickly renewed acquaintance with a young man named Eustace Sloop. Sloop (as I had called him when he was in the academic college) had got his A.B. in 1897 and had then gone off to teach and work in the summers in order to earn money with which to finance his medical studies.

He had come to Davidson back in '93 as the youngest freshman in the class. I well remember him as he was then: a tall, slender, shy youngster with light brown hair and the nicest smile. I thought he was quite good-looking, and I still do, though no longer is he slender and long ago that brown hair turned white. Now, with his grizzled whiskers and goatee, he's a spittin' image of old Dr. Caldwell on the patent-medicine ad. But his nice smile hasn't changed a bit.

Early that freshman year we had had a party at our house for members of the class, and Sloop had come. The principal thing I recall about him that evening was his great interest in an oil painting in the dining room of a bowl of fruit. In those days everybody had a painting of fruit or game over the sideboard. I was glad ours was peaches and bananas and a prickly-looking pineapple, rather than a dead duck with his bloody head·hanging off the table. He showed not a spark of interest in me that night, nor I in him. After all, he was only a very young freshman while I was a lady already graduated from college.

Sloop had been brought up on a farm a few miles east of Mooresville, a small town six miles north of Davidson, and as a child had ridden a mule every morning to school in Mooresville, because at that time there was no high school out in his section. He was a good athlete, and had been captain of a baseball team in his community. He soon earned a place

17

on the Davidson College baseball team and played football as well. I remember that several years ago he was reading an article about some famous man, one of the leading figures, if I recall correctly, in World War II. Suddenly he looked up and smiled. "I remember that fellow," he said. "I played football against him when I was on the Davidson team. He was a good player too, and a wonderful sport. I figured then that some day he'd amount to something."

We had some classes together, but neither of us gave a thought to romance. In fact, in those days I wasn't thinking of getting married. I liked the boys—and still do—but simply as companions, friends to pal around with, and Sloop was just another one of the boys.

Then he was graduated and gone. He taught for a part of the time at Pantops Academy, a preparatory school for the University of Virginia. In the summers he worked on the farm. Every cent he could put by went into the fund to see him through med school.

In the fall of 1902 he was back at Davidson to take medicine. We became classmates a second time. I stopped calling him Sloop and in recognition of his new and more dignified station began to call him Doctor. I've been calling him Doctor ever since. I can't imagine any other name that could possibly fit him.

Doctor had taken a room in his aunt's home next door to ours. Sometimes he'd come over after supper for a while. Father was a popular professor, and often there'd be boys at our house in the evenings. Doctor, whose room was on our side, got to watching for those boys to leave, and after they had gone he would come over to say good night. We were beginning to get interested in each other. Doctor was now a fine-looking young man, nine years older than he had been when he entered Davidson as a very youthful freshman. I was nine years older, too, but I figured they hadn't damaged me too much. I made up my mind that I wasn't going to be

18

one of those college widows, though I might be already headed that way. . . . Isn't it silly how a twenty-nine-year-old girl in this country must consider herself a spinster?

It was during this year that I learned that the church would not accept me as a candidate for the foreign-mission field. They said I was too old—and I was still under thirty!—to learn a foreign language, and to this very final observation they added the declaration that at such an advanced age I wouldn't be physically able to stand the rigors of a tropical country. I wonder what those Presbyterian brethren would think if they knew that fifty years later this old woman could still tramp over the mountains around Crossnore!

After we had finished that first year in the medical school at Davidson—without my being allowed to take anatomy!—I made plans to continue my medical studies at the Woman's Medical College of Pennsylvania, at Philadelphia. Doctor planned to take his second year at Davidson.

That fall I entered the Philadelphia institution and was informed immediately that I would be obliged to double up on my anatomy. I buckled down to hard study and as a result was able to win the prize in that subject, which was a great joy to me and great encouragement, for I was no brilliant student.

Doctor and I wrote each other, and during my years in Philadelphia he came up to see me several times. It was during this time that we became engaged, though just when it was, for the life of me I can't say. It was no cataclysmic event. It wasn't accomplished in the manner of the romantic novels of fifty years ago or the glamorous present-day movies. We seemed just to drift into the sea of matrimony, and, once in it, we've never had any desire to venture out of those waters.

I was graduated from the medical college in 1906, and I chose the New England Hospital for Women and Children, at Boston, for my internship. At the end of that year I was invited to go to Agnes Scott College in Georgia as that institution's first resident physician. It was while I was down there that Doctor was completing his postgraduate course at Jefferson Medical College.

That winter, or spring, perhaps it was, we made a momentous decision. We decided that after we were married in the summer we would settle down in the North Carolina mountains. If we could not be foreign missionaries, we could serve at home.

Several reasons entered into our decision. For one thing, both of us were familiar with the mountains and loved that section. Doctor, in fact, had already begun his practice at a tiny place called Plumtree. During his student days, in the summer after the crops had been laid by, he had gone to the mountains and once had made an extensive walking trip over the region that included Plumtree and Blowing Rock, some twenty-five miles or so apart.

My family had had a summer home at Blowing Rock for many years, but during Mother's illness I hadn't been able to spend much time there. Blowing Rock is now one of the most beautiful and popular resort towns in the mountains. It is visited each summer by thousands of motorists coming along the Blue Ridge Parkway. It gets its name from the Blowing Rock, a cliff towering more than two thousand feet above the Johns River Gorge. From it one has a breath-taking view of the Blue Ridge Mountains. Straight across the gorge lies old Grandfather, serene and ageless. They say that if you throw your handkerchief, or even your hat, over the precipice of Blowing Rock, the upsurge of air currents in the gorge will bring it back to you. I don't know; I'm Scotch.

Our family was one of the first of the outlanders to establish a summer home at Blowing Rock. When Father first began teaching at Davidson College, he felt very keenly the lack of laboratory equipment, especially in geology. So he decided to go into the mountains to hunt geological specimens. He had a cousin preaching at Horseshoe, and this cousin promised to act as guide in his explorations. So they and the professor of physics at Davidson, who had come with Father to the mountains, joined in the hunt for specimens.

Blowing Rock was the place that intrigued them most. Father got many specimens in that area, and he became interested also in the formation of the Blowing Rock itself. He reported his findings to the state geologist, and afterward they came up together and liked the spot so much that they each built a summer home there.

Doctor and I knew that living in the mountains would be different. We were quite sure it would be primitive, and often difficult. We would be denied many things to which we were accustomed. We would enjoy few of even those simple pleasures afforded residents of a small church-college town. There would be long periods of separation from relatives and dear friends and that sense of isolation experienced only by those who live far back in the deep coves. The ache of loneliness would at times sorely trouble us.

But we had wanted to be missionaries, Doctor and I, and what could be better than to spend our lives helping to bring to these people of the mountains, these fine, high-principled men and women so capable of great things, a more fruitful, happier manner of living?

We knew that was what we wanted to do—to live among them, seek to help them, enjoy them, learn from them, become a part of them. And never have we regretted our decision. We have helped them, Doctor and I; but, more than that, they have helped us. We have been the winners.

The wedding, we decided, would be in Blowing Rock, on July 2, 1908. We would go from the family's summer house to the church.

We had planned our honeymoon, too, of course. We would ride farther into the mountains, on horseback, and end our trip at our home. For we had decided also to live at Plumtree. We looked forward to the journey, for I had ridden horseback a great deal and was quite at home in the saddle. I owned a young mare named Beauty—and what a beautiful animal she was! And Doctor, by now, having started his mountain practice, almost lived in the saddle.

# 6

WE were married early in the morning. I can never forget how pretty the little church looked. The Blowing Rock children had decorated it with mountain flowers and evergreens, simply but most effectively, and they had been so interested in doing it.

My pastor, Reverend A. T. Graham, came up from Davidson to perform the ceremony. He was a close friend of the family, and he was also quite fond of Doctor. He has long been dead now, but his widow is still living at ninety-four, an age that would indicate she came of mountain stock, for we have many people in their nineties living in the mountains.

We had no flourishes. We were about to enter upon a pioneer life, and we felt that we should begin it as we expected to live it, simply. There were no attendants. I wore a white linen suit; Doctor had on a black suit. I very distinctly remember cutting it up when Will, our son, was five or six years old to make him a suit and how proud he was that he was going to wear his daddy's wedding suit.

From the church we returned to my brother's house for the wedding breakfast. While we were eating, the children prepared us a noisy surprise. When we came out to mount our horses for the ride around Grandfather to Linville, where we planned to spend our honeymoon, we found the entire countryside's supply of tin cans and cowbells tied to our horses' saddles.

The horses didn't like it; they were shying and prancing, but we managed to get on and keep to our saddles. Then we were off at a gallop, rattling and clanking down the road to the children's great glee.

I had changed to a brown riding habit, made for sidesaddle use, so that one side of the skirt was much longer than the other. Perhaps few young women today would know what one was if they saw it. We got away from Blowing Rock about ten o'clock, but we hadn't ridden long before it began to rain. I had brought along a large cape of the style worn by army officers, and Doctor had a slicker. He had rolled the cape inside the slicker and fastened it to the back of his saddle. We put them on and soon were snug and protected from the downpour.

Toward noon the rain slacked off, and we began to look for a place to stop for our honeymoon picnic. They had packed us a bountiful lunch of fried chicken and country ham, biscuits, pickles, small pies, and other delicacies. Shortly we discovered alongside the road, which was little more than a trail, a large flat rock which would make an ideal place to eat. Doctor dismounted and dropped his horse's reins. Then he helped me off Beauty.

I started to look for a place to tie her.

"There's no need tying her," Doctor said. "I never tie Daisy. I just drop the reins so she can browse, and she waits until I return. I always do that way when I'm making calls."

"But Beauty isn't used to that," I protested. "She might run away."

"Oh, no, she won't," Doctor said, "not with Daisy here to keep her company. She'll be all right. Let's spread the lunch." I figured it wouldn't be too good an idea to argue with him only a few hours after we were married. So we left the horses and went over to the rock and spread out the food. Then we heard a commotion, and looking around we discovered the two horses galloping down the road, Daisy in the lead.

"I'll catch them," Doctor said, setting down the biscuits. "They won't go far. Are you afraid to stay here by yourself?"

"Why, of course not," I said. "But don't be gone long. I'm famished."

But Doctor was gone a long time. When I could no longer hear those horses' hoofs pounding along that narrow road, I knew he was in for a long walk. I waited patiently for a while. Then I leaned back against the sloping rock and closed my eyes, and already the practical mountain housewife, I went to sleep.

When I waked up, Doctor was standing over me. The two horses were a few paces away, both securely tied to saplings. Doctor was grinning. "I'll say you weren't scared!" he observed. Then he told me that two miles down the road a mountain man, a friend of his, had stopped the horses. "He thought they had thrown and maybe killed us," Doctor said. "He knew my horse. He was right worried, too. And all the time you were up here on a rock, asleep." He smiled again, and he looked right proud.

We had our picnic lunch and did well by it, too. With some difficulty I refrained from saying "I told you so" about the horses—and our marriage has been a grand success ever since.

Then we mounted once more and rode toward Grandfather. By the time we came opposite the mountain it was pouring rain again. When we reached Linville's Eseeola Inn, a still famous resort hostelry almost in the shadow of Grandfather, it was almost night. We ate voraciously, and soon after supper went to bed, aching and exhausted.

Our first day of married life, measured by modern honeymoon practices, had been strenuous, exacting, and primitive, but, oh, so happy. Somehow this first day, and the days that were to follow during that week, were to be the gauge of our more-than-twoscore years of living in the mountains.

The next morning—fairly early too, especially for honeymooners—we were in our saddles again. Doctor wanted to introduce me to many of our new neighbors, already his patients. That's what he told me, though I felt, somewhat immodestly, that he just wanted to show off his new bride to them. At any rate, we had an early breakfast and started out.

All day we rode, and over what roads. Present-day North Carolinians, even those living far back in the mountains, can have no idea of the difficulty of traveling in those days, even on horseback. And there was no other way to get around in many sections forty years ago, except to walk. We would strike off through deep forests, tangled with mountain laurel and rhododendron, up the beds of swift mountain streams, around boulders and impenetrable snarls of dank green undergrowth, and after a while come to a cabin clinging to the steep side of the hill or sheltered in a small cove beside a little stream.

The people would welcome us warmly, with an inherent graciousness that immediately disclosed to us that they, though living far back in an isolated region and in primitive conditions hardly understandable even to us of small-country-town rearing, had come of gentle forebears. I could close my eyes and conjure up visions—I had to close my eyes, certainly, in order to do it—of great English stone houses, of lords and ladies having tea on broad terraces, of clipped lawns sweeping away to neat hedges and broad fields stretching beyond. And I could see daring sons of two centuries ago leaving these manor houses, and other homes not so pretentious, to try their fortunes in that strange new country of America.

When I opened my eyes the vision was gone, and I faced the stark reality of a little mountain cabin and the great-great-grandson, perhaps, of one of these venturesome English youths of the early eighteenth century, as he welcomed Doctor and me to his home.

How pitifully primitive were so many of these homes! Some were log cabins, the cracks between the logs chinked with clay and small stones, with one big room and perhaps a shed room attached, and an attic they called the loft, where a half-dozen stalwart boys might sleep. Frequently the cooking was done in the open fireplace.

Other homes were boarded up, sometimes right over the logs. Often we would visit a home in which the cooking was done in this shed room on a cast-iron stove that burned wood. It sat on four curved legs, had an oven at the bottom and three or four openings at the top with covering stove lids. Invariably a kettle, or kittle, as they called it, sat above one of these openings and gave off a gentle singing sound as the water in it boiled away. Sometimes, if the fire was very hot, the lid on the kettle jiggled merrily.

Now and then these homes had sash windows. Others had only wooden shutters that when closed left the interior in deep gloom. Most of them were bare of ornamentation. Often the only coloring within the house was the gay patchwork quilts on the beds and the pages torn from magazines and pasted on the walls to cover the cracks and keep out the frigid winter air.

We visited many such homes during that week of our honeymoon. Each night we would return, weary but happy, to Eseeola Inn and the contrast of elegance—even for that day—of a mountain resort hotel over the drab primitiveness of those little mountain homes. Some nights I lay quiet and wondered. What would the days ahead bring me? Would my life be spent in such a house far back in some isolated valley? Had I turned my back completely upon the life to which I had been accustomed? I had left a cultured home in a friendly little college town, a home of books and music and newspapers and magazines and evenings of good talk and the companionship of interesting people. It is true that I had never been used to much money, but I had had many of the things that, under different circumstances, would have required much money to obtain, and others that money could not have procured.

The Doctor and I could have assured ourselves of such a life by establishing a joint practice in some town or city in our own part of the country. Yet we were leaving this sort of life for one I knew little about, for a life that I was quite certain would be hard most of the time, primitive, often lonely, always challenging.

Challenging. That was it. Sometimes I would be fearful and ready almost to suggest to Doctor that we turn back and ride eastward toward the level country. And then I'd remember that word. We were being challenged. Life was daring us. Life was dealing out the cards. I would pick up my hand and play it. And I'd have fun, too, doing it.

We had little money, but we did have our medical degrees, and we figured we were both pretty good doctors; we had health, we were both as tough as pine knots, and we could take a lot of licks. We could return them, too, in terms of healthy swings at disease and poor diet habits, poverty through lack of opportunity, illiteracy, and all the other ills that were preventing these fine people of the mountains from enjoying the sort of life that their Creator meant for them.

It was a challenge. I knew, that first week of our married life, that first week in the mountains together, that we had come to stay. And I knew that, despite hard days and tough problems ahead, we'd love it.

So we spent our days in the saddle and our nights back at the Eseeola Inn. We rode up and down and across the beautiful Linville Valley, we pushed up the slope to the summit of Grandfather and looked back eastward to the Johns River Gorge and Blowing Rock and on beyond toward the level country of our birth, the land we had left.

The last day of our honeymoon came, and we mounted our horses again and headed west, farther west into the high mountains. The sun was at our backs, the problems and the promise lay before us. We rode steadily toward Plumtree, a tiny settlement named years before for a great plum tree that stood there. We climbed higher in to the mountains, and as we rode, the sun overtook us and passed us, and we rode toward its last rays.

It had dropped low behind the hills when we reached Plumtree and unsaddled our tired horses at our new home.

# 7

IT was certainly no dream house for a brand-new bride to be coming home to, as I very quickly saw. They were building a new dormitory for a boys' school there, and when Doctor told them he was getting married, they hurriedly finished up three rooms on the second floor for our temporary quarters.

This was our new home. It was a strange one, for the rest of the building hadn't even the storm sheeting on it. But after we made our way through the unfinished structure and closed the doors in our little upstairs apartment, we were quite snug and comfortable. Besides, I had little opportunity that first night to get homesick or give consideration to what strange destiny of our own contriving lay ahead. I was simply too sleepy. In our little bedroom perched high up in this skeleton of a boys' dormitory I slept like a newborn baby.

The next morning I was up early and stirring. I wanted to see what Plumtree looked like. It didn't take long, for there wasn't much to see. There still isn't much to Plumtree, although today, in comparison with its size forty years ago, Plumtree is a metropolis. In 1908, it was the center of the mica industry, a sort of headquarters for mining activities. There were two stores, one on each side of the little Estatoe River, which everybody quickly learned to call the 'Toe. A swinging bridge connected the two stores and served to tie the little village together. The stores sold hardware to the miners and each carried a line of staple groceries and dry goods.

From the stores you could see four or five houses, maybe another one or two if you looked carefully. But it was a very small place. There was another building—Doctor's office— only a short distance from our living quarters, nearer the riverbank. Between the steps in front of the office, which were long and quite dilapidated, and the 'Toe River, there was a road. The office building was old and beaten, the ceiling, I discovered the moment I walked in, had begun to drop down in places, and the cobwebs were numberless.

That little office was hopeless; I saw no way of improving it, because it was too far gone. It hadn't been used for years when Doctor took it over, and it hadn't been built as a doctor's office in the first place. Probably it had just been a little two-room home.

We quickly realized that we were beginning a very full life. It might be primitive, but it would never be boresome. From the beginning of our life together, I pitched in and helped Doctor with the practice, though he has always carried the burden of it, especially after the children were born. As the weeks and months went by, more and more people came to that little office and were cordial and glad to see us, and so appreciative of whatever aid we could give them. Often when Doctor was away on long visits on horseback into the mountains—and he made many and long ones—I treated people who came to the office. Frequently I would saddle my horse and go with him on a case, if he planned to operate.

We were not prepared, of course, to do major surgery. Nor had we expected to be more than general practitioners. But when we got to Plumtree, we found few roads open over which patients could be transported to surgeons who were far away. Often surgery was necessary, and surgery in a hurry. So we decided that we must meet circumstances the best way we could.

I well remember the afternoon the first surgical emergency

29

came to us. I was alone in that little shack of an office; looking back, I'm reluctant to call it a shack because so much love and work and faith and hope and praying have been encompassed within those four walls. Doctor was up the river seeing a patient.

Outside I heard the tramp of feet, and I went to the door. A dozen men were coming toward me, four of them carrying on an improvised stretcher a young man who I later discovered was a sturdy, tough-muscled blacksmith. But now he was groaning and writhing with pain. I recognized the old man walking at the head of the little group. At the foot of the high steps to the office he turned around and said to them:

"Put him down, right here."

"What's the trouble, Uncle Pass?" I called down to him.

"He's got somethin' awful wrong in his belly," he said, "and I've seen lots of them die with that. But I b'lieve you could cut him open and take it out, whatever it is. So I brung him to you. Just open him up."

I explained that Doctor was away, but that if they'd bring the patient in, we'd put him on the table and I'd make an examination. It was evidently a ruptured appendix and in bad condition. But what would I do? We had no sterilizer save a tiny instrument sterilizer. We had few instruments. But something had to be done and done right away.

So I left them to watch the suffering young man and went across the little river on the swinging bridge to the store on that side. I told the storekeeper that I needed a fifty-pound lard can, and explained what I was going to do. He said he had nothing empty but he'd empty one for me. So he did, and I bought a ten-cent tin pan and came home with my sterilizer-to-be. Doctor, I thanked Providence, had returned.

We punched holes in the bottom of the lard can and in the top. We put water in the tin pan and placed it on our little two-burner oilstove, and put the sterilizer over one burner and the oven over the other. I put a thermometer in

30

the top of the sterilizer after I had fixed dressings and placed them in it, for I wanted to be certain that the dressings were sterile and the thermometer would tell us when the temperature was sufficient to do the sterilizing.

We had gowns, masks, and things of that sort that we had used in our college courses. I brought them all out. Everything was ready for the operation. Then we moved the patient over into the unfinished dormitory, which we had decided to use as our operating room. We had to put down some boards to provide a flooring, for that part had not been floored. Nor did it yet have walls. It was still simply a skeleton building. But there was a roof over our heads, at any rate.

We had no electric lights, of course. The best light we could afford was supplied by kerosene lamps. Some people had only old-time lanterns. Many a time in the years that were to come Doctor would do major operations by the flickering light of lamps and lanterns.

Well, we made our patient as comfortable as we could and spent most of that night sterilizing our dressings, for our improvised sterilizing equipment would take only a piece or two at a time, and as soon as each batch dried out in the oven we would put in another. On toward daybreak I told Doctor to go to sleep and I'd watch the rest of the night, because he was to do the main operating.

When we went downstairs after daybreak to find how the patient was doing, we found people already collecting—a lot of them—big, strong men, some of them rough-looking, all of them interested in what was going to happen, and many of them opposed to our operating. Several were arguing vehemently with the old father and telling him that he was a fool to let these young doctors practice on his son. "They'll kill him," they said. "He won't never wake up."

But he insisted that it was the only thing that would save the boy. He knew it was, he said, and he wanted it done.

It frightened me a bit to see them come with shotguns and

rifles; but I hadn't been in the mountains long before I learned that the men generally traveled with guns on their shoulders so as to be able to get a shot at a squirrel or a wildcat or anything else that might come along.

The operation went slowly but steadily. It seemed a mighty long time to me. We had found a terrible situation in that abdomen and privately wondered if the young man would live overnight. But we didn't forget what we had been taught to do, nor did we forget how we had been taught to pray. So we went ahead with prayers in our hearts, because we knew it was a crucial time.

The operation was a success. The young man survived the night and quickly began to mend. Within a few weeks he was ready to go back to blacksmithing. But we wouldn't allow that. We made him stay quiet a while longer. That was in the days before surgeons got appendectomy cases on their feet a few hours after surgery.

All of this was new in the Plumtree community. They hadn't been accustomed to anything of the sort. A very few people had been sent way off to some doctor and had had surgical work done. With some the surgery had been successful, with others it hadn't. They didn't know around Plumtree how to trust a surgeon.

But after our success with the young blacksmith, operations became pretty numerous, and I used to laugh and tell Doctor that he was depriving the human body of everything that it could spare and some things I thought it couldn't.

The good Lord took care of us, though, and our patients got well. That made a great deal of friendship for us in Plumtree and even a mite of respect of our work among the neighboring people. Sometimes they came great distances on improvised stretchers or even in oxcarts to have major operations done. It was bad on patients when they were brought in oxcarts, for the roads were rough in those days. We were always glad when they brought them on stretchers.

But this growing confidence in us as doctors served to increase tremendously the task of serving the people of our section of the mountains. As time passed, Doctor's trips away from the office became more numerous, and he had to ride longer and longer distances. I helped as much as I could, but even then it seemed that he would not be able to keep up with his steadily mounting practice. When we learned that our family was to have an addition and the time for the arrival neared, I was able to help less and less.

The baby was a girl and we named her Emma. She is now Mrs. Dwight Fink, a doctor of medicine herself and in charge of our hospital at Crossnore, and a very fine doctor if I do say so myself.

Many were the long nights I was at home alone with the baby as Doctor rode horseback, or led his horse in order to keep warm by walking, on visits to sick or injured people far back in the coves and hills. Sometimes I grew terribly afraid as the hours dragged by and Doctor did not return.

I remember particularly one night that was for me a time of agony of spirit. Doctor had gone across Jonas Ridge and down to his home near Mooresville to see his father, who was ill. He had said that he would be back that night. When he left home the weather was good, but later a blizzard came up. I knew, of course, that he would know nothing of the blizzard when he left his father's home down there to return to the mountains.

The thermometer was dropping with alarming rapidity. The snow blew into drifts, and the wind howled. The men who came to the office and the ones I saw when I went across the little swinging bridge to the store in the early afternoon said to me, "Don't look for Doctor tonight. He can't make it. Nobody could live crossing Jonas Ridge tonight."

And the weather continued to get worse.

But I knew that Doctor would cross Jonas Ridge that night, if he lived. Once he started home he always came. So I couldn't control myself, and I began to worry, even though I tried to exercise faith. Emma was asleep in her little crib; I had been keeping up the fires to warm Doctor when he came. But the wood was getting low; I had burnt it too fast. So, finally, way after midnight, I got in bed to keep warm.

A long time passed. And I went to sleep.

Someone touched me, and quickly I was awake. It was Doctor. I knew then what is the height of joy in this world. I got him warm. He said he had had to walk a long part of the way. His walking had made him late. But the exercise had kept him warm and saved his life.

Those terrible nights did not come often. But one can never forget them. And we're thankful that we were cared for through all of them.

We had another such memorable night coming up from Mooresville. Because the roads had been worked, and it was a dry spell and cold, we got out the old buggy that Doctor had brought up to the mountains—a good one when he bought it, but it had been standing idle so long. In those days we would ride on horseback or in the buggy down to Morganton, some thirty-five or forty miles, and then leave the saddle horses or the horse and buggy there and catch the train to Mooresville. Coming back, we'd get off the train at Morganton, mount our horses or get into the buggy, and journey that way the rest of the distance home.

So this day we got out the old buggy. I had the baby carefully wrapped up, for it was a sharply cold day, and I remember that before we started I was anxious because Doctor had taken a group of youngsters out on the river ice skating, and we were making a later start than I thought was wise.

We got down to Mooresville all right. It was the coming back that even to this day gives me a certain sinking feeling when I recall it.

We came to Morganton on the train, hitched our horse to the buggy, and started north toward Plumtree. It was night when we began climbing Ripshin; we noticed that the cold was becoming more and more bitter, and the wind began to blow, which always adds to trouble. We had no protection whatsoever, for there was no cover on the buggy. The horse's feet slipped occasionally. And I was so afraid that little Emma was getting too cold.

Finally we reached the top of the ridge and approached the little hotel which, appropriately enough for that night, was called Cool Springs Hotel. I knew that the most hospitable people on earth lived right there. So we decided that we'd stop and ask if they'd take us in for the rest of the night; it was already midnight.

We rapped on the door, and they got up and let us in. The house was cold, but in the living room there was still just a little fire. They stirred it up, and we warmed ourselves there. But the wind was still blowing, so they were afraid to have much fire, for fear sparks flying out the chimney might ignite the house. We went to bed in a cold room. Emma didn't seem to mind it, but Doctor and I suffered very much because of the cold that night.

During our conversation with old Mr. Loven, the proprietor, as we hovered over the few coals, I found that he had been a private in the regiment of which my father was the colonel, and he said that his company was thrown very intimately with Father a good deal of the time. He didn't want to go to bed; he wanted to talk about the war, and what Father had done, and how brave he thought Father was, and what a splendid colonel he'd been, and so on. And I, cold as I was, enjoyed hearing it.

The next morning the wind had lulled, the fires were bigger; we got thoroughly warmed and started out. We had little trouble from then on getting home.

Though sometimes I suffered the hardships of traveling in the mountains in winter, it was usually Doctor who braved the cold and the wet day or night to minister to the sick. The roads in those days seemed so frequently to cross the numberless streams. These streams were sometimes out of their banks and swift, especially the 'Toe River, and often it was necessary to ride with your feet sticking out past the horse's neck to keep them from being splashed with icy water which the poor horse was plowing through.

This brings to mind one very cold night when I was anxiously waiting for Doctor to come from a long trip across Grassy Ridge. I knew that as he came down Roaring Creek he had to cross it thirteen times. I knew also that the creek was high. This made it hard for him to walk and warm himself up with the exercise, as he customarily did when he grew so cold from riding in the saddle. He had learned, too, that if he took his feet out of the stirrups they would warm up a little, because the blood could flow more freely in his legs. But in crossing Roaring Creek so often he couldn't get off and on his horse every time. So he would have to take the splash of the water. And of course he couldn't walk across the river.

I knew he had been through much water that night. I had visions of his horse stumbling, of Doctor getting drenched, and of his clothes freezing on him. I hadn't learned then not to worry about the weather and to trust Doctor's skillful care of himself in all sorts of situations. I put in a fearful evening.

Long after midnight I heard him calling me from the yard below, and I went to the window, so grateful to know that at last he was home.

He called up to me, "Would you mind bringing the hammer down? I need it."

I couldn't imagine why he would want the hammer, but I got it and went on out to him.

I found his feet and the stirrups encased in ice; he couldn't get his feet out. So with the hammer I broke the ice and released him. To this day I don't know why his feet had no frostbite, but they hadn't.

36

Dr. Eustace Sloop's powerhouse where he rebuilt and rewound
an old dynamo and brought electricity to Crossnore (*above*).
Grandfather Mountain reflected in a mountain pond (*below*).

Then and Now: (*above*) an early "street," and Crossnore's business center prior to 1918; (*below*) a view of the town today.

The case he had gone to was serious and the patient had needed him, and I was glad he could go. But it was terrible to think of what he had suffered during that trip across Grassy Ridge, for the ridge was high and unprotected and the night had been so bitterly cold.

They finally finished the boys' dormitory, and we moved across the river into a recently vacated cottage, where we built a little office more suitable to our needs. Patients continued to visit us, and often I kept the office and treated the visitors while Doctor was riding the hills and coves and fording the swift mountain streams.

We were busy, and we were very happy—happy at the thought that perhaps we were beginning to fulfill our mission.

# 8

ONE day while we were living at Plumtree they brought a little Negro boy into the office. It was unusual to have a Negro patient; there weren't many colored people in this section. There are comparatively few now, in fact.

This little boy lived four or five miles up the river at a place they called Beech Bottoms. He had got a long gash, from something he had fallen on, right down the middle of his forehead. Doctor put him on the operating table, cleaned out the wound, got everything ready, and told him he was going to be a little man and let him sew that thing up.

"Yas, suh," he said, "I don't mind. I ain't agoin' to holler none."

But Doctor knew the sewing would be painful, and he was puzzled as to what to use. That was a face wound, and he didn't want it to leave an ugly scar. And search all he could, he couldn't find any suitable suture. So he went out to the barn and pulled some long black hairs out of his horse's tail, and these he fetched back to the office. The little Negro boy took a tremendous interest in watching him sterilize those horsehairs.

Then came the sewing. It was accomplished without a great deal of trouble, and the dressings were put on.

"Now remember, in just eight days," Doctor said to the boy—"and that will be such and such a day," he added— "you be sure to come back here and let me take these stitches out."

"Yas, suh, I will," the little Negro assured him. And, with his forehead well bandaged, he went home.

But he didn't come back when the eight days had passed.

"That boy didn't come back to have those stitches taken out," Doctor said to me. And another day passed, and still he hadn't come.

That morning we had a call up the river that necessitated two doctors, and we both went on horseback. There had been a terrible accident at a sawmill. As we were hurrying to this tragedy, we passed a little colored boy sitting on a fence beside the road. It was our little horsehair fellow.

"How's that forehead?" Doctor asked him.

"Fine, Boss," he said, "fine."

"But," Doctor said, "you didn't come and have those stitches taken out."

"No, Boss, it's adoin' so well they don't need to come out."

Doctor said, "Look here, don't you remember that I sewed up that place with horsehair?"

"Yas, suh, yas, suh, and you done a good job too."

Doctor thought for a minute. Then he said: "Well, what are you going to do when one morning you wake up and find a horse's tail growing down the middle of your forehead?"

"Lawd, mister," the little boy shouted, his white eyeballs rolling.

"Well, now, you'd better come down there and have those horsehairs taken out of your skin," Doctor said.

"Yas, suh," he said, "I'll shore be there tomorrow."

But he didn't wait until the next day. When we got back from the trouble up at the sawmill, he was sitting on the steps at the office waiting to have the horsehair stitches taken out.

Not long after Doctor sewed up the little Negro boy's forehead with the horsehair suture, he began going to see a little patient who was not able to come to him.

She lived farther up the mountain than the little Negro boy, and he had arranged to go and see her. It so happened that on that day I couldn't go with him. When he came back, he said that the child was dangerously ill, and that she was going to need a difficult operation before she got any better. She was going downhill pretty fast. His examination had revealed a critical kidney condition.

Her home was way up near the top of Grassy Ridge. I had never been to that place, but I knew that it would be beautiful. I agreed to go with Doctor and help him attempt that operation. He had given the little girl's family instructions about having the kitchen table cleared off and scrubbed and the washpot full of water and boiling by the time we got there, and he had told them we would come the next day.

But that night the thermometers dropped down below zero. All the creeks froze up. Everything was horrible. We couldn't go.

So we waited a few days, worrying all the time about the little girl. And then we got a message that the men would come down the next day, for us to be ready, and that they would break the ice with their axes as they came down; as they went back up, they would break the ice again if any had refrozen. But some help must come quickly for the little girl.

So we sterilized everything, and prepared our dressings. We put them in flour sacks and swung them across our saddles, as we always did, even taking our own pans for the antiseptics. Our little sterilizer for the instruments was a tin pan with a cover to it.

We followed the men up the mountain, a long, hard trip in bitterly cold weather. My little horse stumbled more than Doctor's did, but she never fell. We crossed that creek thirteen times, but we made it. We got a little wet with the splash of the water, but not seriously. High up the slope we ran across some men digging in that frozen ground. They said some rocks had fallen and they had to get the rocks out of the way so we could come by with the horses. This crew of men had been trying to clear the road since early morning.

I liked the look of one man, a young fellow who appeared to be about twenty. He had a very intelligent eye and a kind face, and he attracted me. And, as it turned out, it was lucky we met up with him.

We went along, after a few minutes, to the house. The little mother, who said she had nine children, looked as if she were the older sister of the patient, who was thirteen years old but not big enough for ten. The child looked like a mighty sick one to be operated upon; but something, we saw at once, had to be done, and there was little time to lose.

The washpot was boiling out in the yard, but we didn't dare to work outside that day; it was too cold, and the wind was coming up the valley. So we went into the house, where the kitchen table had been well scoured and fixed ready for us. Some men brought in the washpot, and we began to prepare things. They found us another table, and we put our sterile sheet on it and put out the instruments. Some of them we freshly sterilized in front of the fire.

The little girl was brave as a lion; she was so anxious to get well. We began to operate. But the neighbors kept coming in; they had seen those horses coming up the mountain, and they had followed. They had on dirty, dusty wraps, and since it was cold, they kept them on. I remember especially an old lady with a voluminous cape who insisted upon standing where she could see. I just wondered how many germs were in the air.

They wanted to pick up the instruments and look at them, and I had a time with that. When I'd turn my back on the instrument table and try to help with the operation, I'd hear something, and I knew somebody was fooling with those instruments. So I'd have to scold some more and resterilize.

I thought it was just too trying, too hopeless, to do an abdominal operation in such an infected atmosphere. But I had about gotten them where they'd stand back just a little bit so that we could get light, when all at once there was an awful squawk. An old hen had come in to see what was happening. The door was constantly being opened, and she'd had nothing to prevent her walking in. Somebody thought she ought to get out, and so kicked her.

She rose in the air with a frightening squawk, and she settled down right on the little girl's abdomen and cocked her head to one side and looked down into the wound!

And then she flew off.

I just knew that child would die. I just knew it.

When we had got about half through the operation, the little girl collapsed, and we had to begin reviving measures. The young mother, who had undertaken to give the ether and felt sure she could, also collapsed. So I led her out, and she picked up two of the babies as she went, and I took her around to a sunny place in the warm chimney corner, where they were away from the wind. She just sat there moaning as though she were singing a song.

I had come back in to help. Then I went out to her again because it looked, just before we finished the operation, as if the little girl might go. So while Doctor was giving the small patient a stimulant, I went out to the mother and said, "I believe it would be better if you'd come inside."

She said, "Is she dead?"

"No," I said, "but she's not very far from it."

And with that same mournful moan she brought the two children in and sat down.

Somehow, in spite of everything, the little girl revived. After hours of breathless watching, we saw that she was rallying and decided that we could go home. Before leaving, we gave written instructions to the boy with the intelligent face we had met coming up the mountain. He had followed us up and had been helping with the operation. It turned out that he could read, a discovery which pleased us a great deal, for it was quite possible that he was the only person in that room besides Doctor and me who could read "writin'." Most of those present were adults, but illiteracy among them was frightful in those days. Some boasted of the ability to read "printin'," though handwriting, they admitted, was too much for them.

We wrote the instructions in a careful, big hand and read them over several times to the boy who could read. He was sure he could handle the situation.

It was a terrible night. Two or three times my horse turned —just whirled around—and refused to face the wind. Doctor would get far ahead of me; I could still see his lantern, but I could not make him hear me. Then he would notice that I was not behind, especially when he went into the creek and did not hear my splash behind him. Then he'd turn around and wait for me. I'd get my horse persuaded, and down the hill we'd go again. We'd cross the creek, and I'd keep count to see how many more times we'd have to cross.

But we did get home. Nothing had hurt us. We thawed out, and after a few hours' sleep we were all right.

Several days later Doctor went up on the mountain to see the little girl. Every day they had sent a messenger down to tell us how she was, and we were so pleased to hear that she seemed to be improving.

Doctor discovered, when he got up there to see her, that the improvement was very real.

Then it was a week or two before he went again, and she

told him she was about well. Exactly six weeks after that operation we came back one day from a trip, and there sitting on the steps waiting for us was this little girl.

"I walked every foot of the way! I stopped at Mandy's house and rested awhile," she said, "but I walked every foot of the way!" She was beaming.

Conveyances weren't usable at that time of the year in that country, and she said she hadn't wanted to get on horseback, which was probably a wise decision.

The last time I heard of that little girl she was not only married but was the model housekeeper in her settlement—and had ten children!

## 9

RECALLING our experiences of practicing medicine during the time at Plumtree inevitably brings to mind a woman who came across the mountain one day to see us. She had not been well for some time, she said, and this day she was complaining of a great deal of pain in the abdominal region.

"I got a risin' in my side down here," she said, touching the place gingerly. "It's apainin' me terrible, and it's agrowin'. I want you to do somethin' for me."

Doctor examined her, and decided that she should have a difficult surgical operation. He persuaded her to go to Statesville, a town about a hundred miles away, and have the operation done there by a noted surgeon.

It was a terrible trip over rough roads, but she stood it. The surgeon examined her, agreed with Dr. Sloop's diagnosis, and undertook to operate; but he found in the intestines an advanced cancer that he considered inoperable. So he refused to go further, and sent her back home. He wrote us that he considered the case hopeless from a surgical point of view, and that he feared she didn't have very long to live. He had made an exploratory operation, he explained, and had then sewed her up without attempting to remove the cancer.

We didn't know anything to do, but we hated to tell her what the surgeon had said. It was apparent that she thought he had operated upon her, and she seemed quite cheerful.

Doctor and I talked it over. I remembered that in my work as an intern I had seen one of our doctors treat some inoperable cases with a certain medicine that seemed to shrink up the cancers. Sometimes the medicine gave the patient a longer life and more comfort. I suggested that we try that medicine.

My husband laughed at me. "I've never practiced hoodoo medicine," he said. "But, if that's what they taught you in Philadelphia, then I'm willing to try it. Certainly it can't do her any harm."

So we tried it. I found the prescription, wrote it out for her, and she got the medicine, which is called methylene blue. Occasionally we heard from her. She reported slow improvement, until finally she was able to be up and about. Soon she was going on with her usual work.

Then one day she was back. "I run out of that blue medicine," she said. "I want another bunch of it." She always said "bunch." She fingered the place again. "That risin' is acomin' back on me. It's painin' me again. Till I run out of that blue medicine it was agoin' down and it wasn't apainin' me. But I been out a while and now it's agrowin' again."

She got another supply of the medicine and went home. She had ridden across the mountain on horseback.

We heard little from her for months—maybe a year.

Then one cold day in the middle of the winter she came again.

"I come back for another bunch o' that blue medicine," she said. "The risin's acomin' back on me again. It's agrowin' too. I been havin' a lot o' misery."

44

"Why didn't you come back for more medicine before you ran out?" I asked her.

She grinned. "Well, Mis' Sloops," she answered, "I wouldn'ta run out yet if it hadn't been for my young 'uns. You gave me a big bunch that last time. But we wuz agoin' to have some company for Christmas and the young 'uns thought it looked mighty bad round the fireplace—all smoked up, you know. So them young 'uns noticed that when I took that medicine in water the water turned blue, and you know what they done? They took the rest o' my medicine and mixed it up in some water and painted round the fireplace with it. That's just what they done. And the risin's acomin' back. So I come back here to get another bunch o' that there medicine."

Now—some forty years later—she's still living, an old lady nearing ninety. Occasionally she takes a little of her blue medicine. She always knows that she has some trouble in her side. But nevertheless she's alive and active, and she says, as a test of her strength, "I'm still able to hoe my cawn." Now she's about as dried up all over, I'd say, as the cancer she's been having for forty years or longer.

We have had one other case in which the methylene blue was used with success in the treatment of cancer. But, as Doctor always hastens to point out, it's a very long chance that my "hoodoo medicine" will be of much help.

10

FROM the time that we settled at Plumtree our practice was heavy. But it continued to grow, and soon Doctor's medical work was taking all his waking moments, and often he got precious few hours in twenty-four to sleep. He had to cover such a wide area, and there was always so much riding, and it took so long to make the visits far back into the isolated areas.

Much of Doctor's practice was over east in the Linville Valley section and beyond, even past Jonas Ridge toward Morganton. Plumtree, we began to discover, was off-center, and that meant that Doctor, and I too quite often, had to ride in the course of a week many miles farther than we would have if we had selected a home east of Plumtree.

The need for a doctor in the Linville Valley was becoming insistent, as Doctor's friends in that region sought to show him. They urged us to move to Crossnore. One of these friends was Mr. Alexander Johnson. Few people knew him by that name, however. To virtually everybody he was Uncle Alex.

Uncle Alex was a mountain man. He had the virtues of the men of the mountains without their failings. He was of medium build and had black hair; he was fast-talking, and fast-walking in his knee-high boots, and an inveterate smoker who could light his pipe in the strongest wind. All who knew him revere his memory. Uncle Alex was a kind and generous father, an exemplary citizen, a wonderful neighbor. "Everything I have is for my neighbors and myself," he used to say, and he meant it.

Uncle Alex insisted that we move to Crossnore. "If you'll just come, I'll move you," he said. And though we had few possessions, it was still a difficult task to move a family over six or seven miles of mountain trails—they were hardly roads in those days—and few vehicles could stand the jolting.

We decided to move. Uncle Alex sent his son Lambert, then a youngster in his early teens, with oxen yoked to a sturdy cart, and Lambert moved us to Crossnore.

It was a dreary, cold afternoon in winter—I'll never forget the date, Friday, December 11, 1911—when we reached our new home, a cottage perhaps half a mile from the little level circle of land on which old George Crossnore had built his store, the small flat that is still the center of our village.

46

Crossnore forty years ago hadn't grown much larger than it was in the days of its founder. Down in the village one could count three houses, a combination schoolhouse-and-church, and one store. The census of 1910 and again the census of 1920 gave Crossnore an official population of 23. The last time I asked Doctor what the population was, he told me, I believe, that it was 282. "It may be 283," he added. "Jim's wife had a new baby this morning." But any way you figure it, Crossnore has had a marvelous growth in thirty years. What other place has grown more than 1200 per cent in that short time?

That store—and I'll never forget it—had two parts. The front part was about fifteen feet square. It was crammed with all sorts of merchandise on and under the counters, on the shelves, against the walls; and I can yet remember those strange and intriguing odors that came from rounds of strong cheese, plug tobacco, coffee, fat back, dried beans, bucket candies, plowpoints, nails, dry goods, and a veritable multitude of oddly assorted merchandise. That was the front part, as I said.

Behind was the post office. The merchant who ran the store was also the postmaster and received and handed out the mail. He came as near to being Uncle Sam as anybody Crossnore boasted.

If you walked out of the store and paused in the front door to look west, you could in that day see two small houses. In one of these lived a father and all except one of his children. The eldest child, a son, and this son's family lived in the other. These houses were two or three hundred yards from the store. In the opposite direction was a little white-painted cottage. It had a small front porch, and the ceiling of the porch, I distinctly recall, was painted blue to represent the mountain sky. In it lived a beloved old couple, Uncle Harve Clark and Aunt Kitty.

Uncle Harve was Uncle Newt's younger brother. Although

47

he was then an old man, he was called "Young Harve" because he had an Uncle Harve who was much older than he, as a long white beard demonstrated. Uncle Young Harve was quite a character himself; I remember that some years after we moved to Crossnore I was sitting beside him one day in court. I had gone there, in fact, to prosecute two of his sons for moonshining (a subject I will get around to later). While we waited for the court to convene, we talked. "Lady," Uncle Harve said to me, "something has happened to me since the last time you saw me."

"What, Uncle Harve?" I asked.

"I've had my seventy-fifth birthday and my seventy-fifth grandchild."

But the most interesting of the buildings at Crossnore was the old structure, straight across from the store–post office, which served as a schoolhouse, church, and magistrate's courtroom for the whole region. No one seemed to know exactly how old it was, but generations had gone to school there, and certainly its appearance indicated it had been built of materials from the Ark. It was little more than a shed. Whether it had originally been built for a schoolhouse they didn't know. But they thought it had—more than forty years ago, they generally agreed—because their parents and grandparents had gone to school there. It was a log house that later on had been planked up on the outside to improve its looks. But it hadn't. Years ago the planks had warped, and now it looked worse than ever.

I was to learn more about it, however, the first Sunday we were in Crossnore, for we went there to Sunday school. Doctor was free that morning because the folks in the vicinity hadn't learned that we had moved to Crossnore. Sundays at Plumtree, and thereafter at Crossnore, were very busy days with him because on Sundays the people had time to go in search of a doctor.

But this first Sunday in our new home he went with me

and carried Emma, who was then still a baby. I remember there had been a heavy snowfall and it was cold. We sloshed through the snow, and after a while we got there and pushed inside the dilapidated old structure, where we found sixty-four other people, some of whom had walked two or three miles and carried babies.

That's the first time I saw the inside of the building. And what I saw was hardly inviting either to worship or to study.

It was dark and gloomy; it would have been so even on a bright day. The boards covering the logs were old, unpainted, and very dark. The ceiling, of old-fashioned beaded cut, had pulled loose from the nails in many places, and the boards were hanging down. They were black with the smoke of leaky stovepipes that went up and across from a battered old wood stove and were held in place by wires strung down from the ceiling. There were glass windows, but not enough to provide adequate lighting. Many of the panes had been broken, and now paper pasted to the sash to keep out the cold also kept out most of the light.

The seats were homemade desks of crudest design and construction. Little tots sat with their feet inches above the floor, while long, gangling mountain youths had to sprawl with their feet under neighbors' desks. But what we noticed most about the desks was the carving. It was evident that artists with pocketknives had done their best, or worst, on those desks. Initials were cut into the tops, the sides, and the backs. The edges had been notched and corners rounded. Some of the knifework had been the labor of love, for Romeos had memorialized their Juliets with initials within interlocking hearts.

They were an attentive group there that Sunday morning. The man who taught the lesson was in dead earnest, we quickly realized, and so were his pupils. He taught the adult class, men and women crowded in one corner of the old structure, and he was also superintendent of the Sunday school.

49

He was a thin, pale, unhealthy-looking man, but he did not lack energy or faithfulness. He was then in his thirties, and already he had a growing family that soon totaled ten children.

I was impressed with him. For one thing, he was clean-shaven, which could not be said of a great many of the men of the community. And he tried so hard to make the lesson clear. But the thing that made my heart ache was the realization that he and his pupils did not know how to get the most out of their Bibles. Evidently there were comparatively few Bibles, and there seemed to be no Bible commentaries that would help them understand the text. From time to time during the lesson when something was referred to, I looked it up in my Bible, and they noticed it and said right straight, "Where did you get a Bible like that?"

"This is an Oxford teacher's Bible," I said. "It has lots of helps in it that show you what the Bible verses mean. It is the kind of Bible that will help you a lot in studying your Sunday-school lessons." I showed them how the references in the back explained the text, how they made the whole story more understandable. And immediately they were interested in my Bible.

There was another class in that Sunday school for the little children, perhaps up to twelve years of age. All the older ones were in the adult class. Lilly Clark taught the youngsters, who were grouped in another corner of the room. There was quite a buzzing as the two teachers and the two groups of pupils talked within this one room, but everyone got along, and one class didn't disturb the other too much.

Each child was given a little picture card of the type given out to Sunday-school children of that day. It had on one side a picture in color, perhaps of Jesus with some of the apostles or some other character or group of characters of Bible times, and a few verses from the Scriptures, including the theme verse, which was called the Golden Text. Usually on the reverse side would be the Bible story for that day. Because they received these little picture cards, the children were known as members of the card class.

After the two classes had completed their lesson, they customarily came together for the closing exercise, which was the reciting by each person present of a memory verse from the Bible. Some had learned verses not too familiar even to students of the Bible; others said ones that were well known. One young man was clever enough to have memorized a long chapter, and he said every word of it without error.

When this phase of the program had been completed, they began to crowd around me to have another look at my Bible. Many of them, grown men and women, parents of large families, could not read or write, I was reasonably certain. Others could read, but not well. But all of them seemed interested. I asked them if they'd like to have a Bible like mine.

Oh my, they would!

I said, "Well, now down home where I was brought up, if you said two hundred verses of Scripture perfectly, you would be given a Bible. It was not quite as good a Bible as this one. But I'll give anybody a Bible just like this who will repeat to me two hundred verses of Scripture perfectly."

Someone asked if it would be necessary to say the two hundred all at once.

"No," I said, "you can say them in lots of fifty or one hundred."

Several of them said they'd try.

Then we went on with the remainder of the service. There hadn't been many men and older boys in the congregation that morning, but now they began coming in. They were wearing heavy leather boots, many of them with spurs, for all men rode horseback in those days, and they rode with spurs. Their tramping in made quite a commotion.

When they had quieted down, the superintendent got up and went to the rostrum. From a shelf he took down the

51

Sunday-school literature to be distributed, including little printed sheets giving information concerning next Sunday's lesson text. He also handed out several quarterlies, though there were not enough to go around, and he made the statement that more money was needed in order to buy more quarterlies, which contained the lessons for three-month periods. Then he gave out the picture cards, one to each child present.

I wondered where they were getting the money with which to purchase these Sunday-school helps. In the short time we had been in the mountains it had been demonstrated to us that we were living among the most independent citizens that could be found anywhere. They believed in helping your brother and your home community particularly, but they believed too in doing things for themselves. They belonged to a regularly organized church—one of the prominent denominations in our state—and they knew that there was a central office of their church organization in Raleigh. They knew that they could write to that office and ask for help in buying literature for their Sunday school, for theirs was a home-mission church and they had services only once a month. The preacher lived nearly forty miles away and came only if the weather was good.

But they had not written to Raleigh for aid. And I soon learned why. It was against their grain to seek outside help. They were just too independent. And I admired them for it.

Now that the Sunday-school superintendent had finished giving out the cards and the other helps, I was to learn quickly, too, how they got the money with which these things were bought. For he walked over to the picture roll hanging at the back of the pulpit. The picture on top illustrated that Sunday's lesson. It was beautifully colored and must have cost quite a sum, I suspected.

He tore off the picture. He did it very skillfully: he ran his knife across the top, and then with a flourish he jerked the picture so that it tore straight across along the line of the cut. Then he turned around to face us.

"We've got a beautiful picture today," he said. He made a little speech about it, calling attention to the characters and the colors, and then he held it up and said, "Who bids?"

One man said, "Five cents."

"Six," another said.

Then everything waked up, and that was the liveliest bidding you ever heard in your life. The picture finally went for forty-four cents. The man who bought it came up to us afterwards to show it off and have a friendly little chat. He was beaming.

"You know," he said, "I aim to buy every one of them pictures. They all fuss because I get 'em, but I save up enough to run it up above anybody else. I've got nine of them already. I aim to get enough to paper the walls of my big room."

Before we left that day, we talked with the thin, pale superintendent. "If you need more quarterlies," I said, "don't you think that the Home Mission Board would give them to you?"

"Well, we ain't never thought that we ought to ask for things like that," the superintendent said. "If they bid pretty well, we get more than enough to buy the roll pictures and the picture cards and helps, and we just put the rest on quarterlies as far as it goes."

And that, I learned, was the way they got the money for conducting their Sunday school.

Not long after that first Sunday I had a visitor. She was Lilly Clark, the teacher of the children's class, and she had come to recite her Bible verses. She said she was a powerful-busy woman and she didn't see any reason why she should come two times, so she'd just say her two hundred verses at one time. She did just that. Another one came within the next day or so. He was a young boy, and he had memorized his two hundred. And when I started to hear him say them,

53

he asked, "Do you mind if I stand up to say 'em? I ain't never practiced 'em asittin' down."

I said, "No, I don't mind at all if you stand up."

He'd had no guidance in the selection of verses to be memorized. I should perhaps have helped him and the others in choosing the verses, but I hadn't, and I was interested in knowing what they had selected. The young woman had made an excellent choice, but this boy had chosen reams of genealogy. He seemed to be fascinated by the word "begat." He reeled off those genealogical passages one after another.

"'And Adam lived a hundred and thirty years, and begat a son in his own likeness, after his image: and called his name Seth,'" the boy quoted from Genesis:

"'And the days of Adam after he had begotten Seth were eight hundred years: and he begat sons and daughters:

"'And all the days that Adam lived were nine hundred and thirty years: and he died.

"'And Seth lived an hundred and five years, and begat Enos:

"'And Seth lived after he begat Enos eight hundred and seven years, and begat sons and daughters: and all the days of Seth were nine hundred and twelve years: and he died.'"

The boy paused, and I thought that now perhaps his recital of the marvelous multitude of days of our first ancestors had come to an end. But no, he shifted his weight to his other leg and started again:

"'And Enos lived ninety years, and begat Cainan:

"'And Enos lived after he begat Cainan eight hundred and fifteen years, and begat sons and daughters:

"'And all the days of Enos were nine hundred and five years: and he died.

"'And Cainan lived seventy years, and begat Mahalaleel'—"

He had slowed over this name, and I looked at the text, for I had opened the Bible at Genesis 5 and had been following

54

him. I didn't offer to correct his pronunciation; I figured his was as good as mine would have been, for I had never heard of this particular descendant of Adam. So, having caught his breath, he went on:

" 'And Cainan lived after he begat Mahalaleel eight hundred and forty years, and begat sons and daughters:

" 'And all the days of Cainan'—"

It was marvelous. I wondered how long it would go on and when he would reach Methuselah, the only one of my ancient fathers I could remember and whose name I could pronounce. Would he get to Methuselah?

He did. It wasn't long before he reached the oldest man. Mahalaleel begat Jared, and Jared begat Enoch, and Enoch begat Methuselah.

Then I learned, for the first time since I had been a child, just how old Methuselah lived to be: " 'And all the days of Methuselah,' " the boy quoted, " 'were nine hundred sixty and nine years: and he died.' "

But not even then did the procession of begats end. The boy was not to stop until Noah had begat Shem, Ham, and Japheth.

He went right on until he had said his verses and qualified for the Bible. Such earnestness I had never seen before. That boy became one of the most purposeful Christians I have ever known. I heard that afterward he had become a minister.

## 11

WHEN Doctor and I came to Crossnore, we were already interested in the education of the mountain children, for the schools were nearly all one-teacher public schools, and often you couldn't find a teacher who had really been trained to teach.

We had found here a people in this Linville Valley, nearly

all of whom were descended from inhabitants of the British Isles, who had kept in contact with their relatives over in the Old Country. Their American forefathers had come into this region before the Revolutionary War, and nearly all of them had ancestors who had fought in that war. A great many of the old men had known Revolutionary soldiers who had lived for years after the Battle of Kings Mountain, in which all of them had taken part and most of them had been wounded.

Hunger for learning, the desire to obtain for their children a better education than they were getting in the one-teacher schools—and some of them were not going to school at all— was very keen in these mountain people. Many of them were immediately interested when we began to talk about improving the school. It took a couple of years though to persuade them that we couldn't do any good toward improving these schools unless we improved the teachers. We talked to them about having teachers who had college educations, and so would be capable of teaching in a way that the local young people, who had only finished a few grades themselves, could not.

First we suggested to the Crossnore people that they needed a certain number of children present before they could get an additional teacher from the State Board of Education, and we insisted that our school must have two teachers, for one teacher could not teach so many grades.

So we preached perfect school attendance—coming every day—as we went about the community and into the homes in our medical work. Soon the number of children increased until we were able to ask the State Board for two teachers and get them.

But that old school building, where we had attended Sunday school on our first Sunday at Crossnore, had but one room, the large one that served as school, church, and courtroom. Nor did the county authorities, whose duty it was to provide the physical facilities for the school, feel that they could offer Crossnore a new schoolhouse. So we went through one year with two teachers doing their best to teach in that one room.

The old structure was even less adaptable to school needs than it was to church purposes. It was dark, as I said, and the children could hardly see to read, particularly the ones seated near the center of the room and farthest from the windows, which on even bright days provided little light. And what was worse, it would take much work on it, a major renovation job, if it was to meet even minimum standards.

So Doctor and I, with several others, decided that we would get all the people together and talk to them about a new schoolhouse. Those mass meetings we held back in the early days were made possible by messages sent around from one neighbor to another: "Tell everybody to come. We're going to have a mass meeting and talk about getting a better school." Those relayed messages brought crowds. Men, women, children, even nursing babies, came to this meeting.

I well remember it. Most of the people wanted a new schoolhouse, we soon saw. But not all of them . . . Paw and Maw had gone to school in the old building, and they had got along all right, and they themselves had gone there, and it would do for the young 'uns. They could get a lot of l'arnin' in the old building. There just weren't no use fer them Sloops to be atryin' to start nothin' fancy around Crossnore. They hadn't been alivin' in this country long enough nohow to l'arn that Crossnore folks didn't hanker after no fancy doin's. The old schoolhouse had been aservin' a long spell now, and twon't no good reason why it couldn't keep on aservin'. . . .

But that group did not prevail. The majority wanted their children to enjoy better opportunities than they themselves had had. They decided we'd build.

Then came up the question of where to put the new building. We talked it up and down. Many of them wanted it built where the old building then stood. It mustn't be moved, they

57

said, for their grandparents had gone to school there, and there it must stay. But I said, "It's right at the crossroads and that makes it dangerous for the children out at play, because of the traffic that passes by."

One old lady spoke up and said, "Sister, don't worry none about that. Oxen ain't bad about runnin' over young 'uns."

So we had to consent to the building of the new schoolhouse on the site of the old one.

But I didn't want that old building torn down. I wanted to use it for something more advanced in education than they had ever had in that valley before. That was a course in manual training, that the men and boys might have some training in carpentry—and then they would be able to build better homes for themselves and for others.

So we talked about it, and we decided to move the old building across the road to the side of the creek and convert it into a manual-training shop. I already had in mind who would teach that class. A boy living not far away had been to Berea College and had learned a good deal about carpentry, and I thought I would be able to get him to teach the course. And that's the way it turned out.

So, having decided to move the old structure, we got two of the best workmen in the group to go out and look and see if that old log house could be moved without falling down. They decided that it could be put on skids and pulled over to the proposed site. So Uncle Alex, who was always eager to have his children obtain an education, said that he would come and put it up on skids, with the help of a few neighbors. Next Monday morning we'd meet there and hitch seven yoke of oxen to it and pull it across the road. It was their decision that it would take seven yoke—fourteen oxen—to pull a thing of that weight.

So the word went out. I had urged them to tell everybody to come, that it would be a great day in education, that we were going to start a school that would become a graded school. Everywhere in that community they were talking and talking about a graded school.

That was in 1913—in the spring, more than a year after we had come to Crossnore. It was the beginning of the new era of better education which has resulted in the Crossnore of today.

Monday morning came, and with an excitement we couldn't conceal we went down to see the old schoolhouse moved across the little flat. I was carrying Emma, who was still a baby. The place was covered with people. They had come from everywhere. They ranged up the hillside and flowed down into the level. And they were all eager to see, and excited. The seven yoke of oxen were standing by meekly, and the old schoolhouse was on skids.

They hooked up the oxen, two behind two, tandem-style. The first thing to do to get them moving was to crack the whip; that was the signal for them to start. Everything now was ready, and somebody nodded to Uncle Bert to proceed.

Uncle Bert Aldridge was the champion whipcracker in all that country. He was a tall, mustached man with dark hair, and he generally wore a cap. His pants legs were tucked into knee boots, and he stood straight-shouldered and erect. He usually talked fast and often in a loud voice, and it was suggested that at times he found it necessary in addressing his oxen to use language hardly suited to the presence of ladies.

Now Uncle Bert was standing ready, his whip grasped firmly in hand. The whip, I must explain, was not meant to strike the oxen; it never touched them, in fact. The trick was to crack it just above their heads and thereby signal them to go forward.

I noticed that old Uncle Preston Johnson, one of the men in charge of the doings, seemed to be regarding me somewhat disapprovingly; but he didn't say anything.

Then Uncle Bert cracked the whip. It sounded like a pistol shot. But instead of going forward, those oxen all tried to go in different directions. They got themselves all entangled in the simple harness. In a few seconds it was all confusion. The house did not budge an inch.

The trouble was that they had never been taught to work in tandem, I figured, and they didn't like those oxen in front of them nor those behind. So they carried on at a dreadful rate.

I was still standing nearby, my baby in my arms, eagerly watching. Most of the women were on the hillside or had retired to the post-office steps a little distance away. One of them came running up to me.

"You're agoin' to get this young 'un killed," she shouted. "You'd better get back out of the way of these here oxen afore they bolt."

"I'm anxious to see an ox move as fast as I can run," I said. "I'm not afraid one bit, and I'm going to stay right here."

"Then I'm not agoin' to let the young 'un be killed," she said, and she grabbed my baby and went running to the post-office steps.

Each of the men who owned a yoke of steers then went up to them and began to talk to them, and smooth their ears. I wondered why they smoothed their ears, but they did—stroking them gently. Then they began to line up the oxen again for another try at moving the schoolhouse.

About that time Uncle Preston came over to me. He was a tall man too, and he stood up straight and square-shouldered. "Mis' Sloop," he said, and his clear blue eyes were serious, "we hate to say this to you, but would you mind agoin' up on that there hill and awatchin' from there?" He spoke in a quick, somewhat shrill voice.

"I'm not afraid of those oxen, Uncle Preston," I assured him. "I know I can go faster than any ox I ever saw."

He didn't say anything, but I saw as he walked away that he seemed displeased.

60

Again Uncle Bert cracked his whip. And again those oxen went in every direction but forward—worse than they had done before. I thought that if that was all the cooperation we would get out of the people, then we were going to have a hard time building the schoolhouse. But it proved the other way around. The people were cooperative; the oxen were not —until something happened.

Once more there was a conference among the owners of the oxen. I was afraid they were going to give up and quit. As they went about the job of trying to straighten out the entangled oxen, I noticed now and then they'd glance at me. Then once more Uncle Preston came over to me.

"Mis' Sloop," he said, "I do hate to say this to you. But we just have to ask you, please, ma'am, to go up there a little ways on the hill and do your watchin' from there."

"I told you that I was not afraid of these oxen, Uncle Preston," I said. "I just know I can go faster than any ox I ever saw."

It was evident that Uncle Preston was embarrassed. He twisted a bit on his feet, swallowed. But his blue eyes were insistent. "Well, Mis' Sloop, ma'am," he said after a moment, "it ain't exactly that. You see we got to git them oxen apullin' straight ahead if we're agoin' to move this here schoolhouse, and you see them oxen don't understand what to do when we speak to 'em in the language we have to use when you're around."

I couldn't argue further. I retired forthwith up the hill. They got the oxen straightened out again and lined up for Uncle Bert to give the signal once more, each man talking into the ears of his oxen. Uncle Bert cracked the whip—and this time the animals plunged straight forward without a hitch. The old building quickly was landed on its new site.

I went home and told Doctor that I never would know what to say to an ox to make him behave, but I'd seen it done.

## 12

SO now, thanks to the effective words of Uncle Preston and the other drivers of the oxen and the last-minute cooperation of the beasts themselves, we had the old house across the flat. The place where it had sat for forty years or longer was now ready as the site of the new school.

The thing to do now was to start work on plans for getting the new school built as quickly as possible. We started right to work and we worked hard. We canvassed the community and talked with the people about giving free labor toward building the two-room structure. The county authorities had agreed to provide half the cost, and it was up to the Crossnore folks to supply the other half. We asked for free lumber, and many agreed to contribute. Education was moving forward at Crossnore. We had visions of a great new day ahead for the people of the Linville Valley.

But it wasn't all accomplished in apple-pie order. There was opposition. Some folks continued to suggest that "them Sloops is atryin' to run things mighty quick seein' as how they is new 'round Crossnore." We even got an occasional anonymous letter. One of these letters, I recall, suggested that "if you don't stop that foolishness about a new schoolhouse you just might get a hole in your back."

I put out the word (I had a good idea who had written the letter) that I'd just as soon go to heaven with a hole in my back as with one in my front. I knew nobody was going to shoot me in the back. I knew folks didn't do things that way in the mountains, not the folks around Crossnore. It was just a bluff to get us to stop pushing for a new school building.

The new schoolhouse would be a simple frame structure, but for our community in that day it would be considered a fine one. The whole community worked on the project, with very few exceptions. Some of our citizens contributed timber, as I've said. We went into the woods and cut down the trees and the oxen pulled them to the sawmill, where they were cut into lumber. When the lumber was properly dried, we started construction.

Many people worked on that building, including the women. I remember how some of our women helped unload the wagons that brought the lumber so that the men wouldn't have to stop carpentering. With all that cooperation and free labor the two-room schoolhouse was finished quickly and everybody was happy.

But what of the furnishings? What would we do for desks and tables and such things?

We moved the old desks from the schoolhouse that the oxen had pulled across the village flat and set them up in the new building. They looked even worse in the new schoolhouse than they had in the old. But they were sturdy, and they would serve until we could do better. For the teachers' tables and other school furniture we put our carpenters back to work, and they made what we had to have. So now we had a new school, furnished and ready for the children—two average-size schoolrooms with a good roof over them, sound walls to keep out the cold, and plenty of windows to let in the light. Something Crossnore had never had before. And we started school.

But almost before we had gotten into the first term, the new schoolhouse was overflowing with children. We saw at once the pressing need for a third teacher. We made a careful count of pupils and discovered sadly that we lacked just two or three of having enough to make us eligible for that third teacher. Nor did we have the third schoolroom, of course.

In those days the school term provided by the state and county was only four months a year. But we had already lengthened our school term to nine months by making the last five months a subscription school and keeping just one teacher to teach from the fourth grade up. A subscription school was one in which the financing was done through the subscriptions of people of the community. In other words, we canvassed the town and raised the money to pay the teachers for those five months and also the expenses of the school during that time, including such things as the cost of fuel.

In an effort to get the children ready for high school (and already we were talking high school as a preparation for college) we struggled manfully through those long winter months. Many pupils of that day—and this was almost forty years ago, remember—quit school about the fourth grade. Few if any compulsory-school-attendance laws were on the books, and for years after we had such laws there was virtually no enforcement of them. But we urged the pupils to continue their studies, and through our efforts a number were persuaded to do so.

As we made progress, the enthusiasm for education grew. Many people who had shown small interest were now looking forward to having their children go on in their studies, and some even expressed the hope that their offspring might have the opportunity of going off to college. So, as I saw the community interest in schooling develop, I said to them, "Now, we just must have three teachers this next year. Already there're too many pupils for two teachers to teach properly."

I kept preaching three teachers. Finally I said to them, "Though we don't have enough pupils, according to the survey, to require the authorities to give us three teachers next year, if you will build the third room, giving your lumber and materials and labor to it, then I'll pay the salary of the extra teacher. But that's all I'll be able to do. That's all the money I'll be able to raise."

They agreed to my proposition. They said they'd get up the lumber and build the third room. And they went to work with energy. Once more the community was cooperating to promote public education.

Every morning Uncle Alex would come. He never failed. The others made him their foreman. And they were faithful, too. Different ones came on different mornings, but every day somebody showed up—usually several persons—and the building kept growing.

After a while the roof was on, the ceiling was in, the flooring was down; everything was finished except the doors and windows.

Then one evening late three of the men, including Uncle Alex, came up to my house to see me, and they were sorely troubled. I asked them why. They answered their trouble was that they couldn't manage the money for the doors and windows.

"I've been wondering," I said, "how you got the money for the nails. You didn't ask me to help you with the buying of those nails."

"No," Uncle Alex said, "we just every mornin' took up a collection from the men that were agoin' to work, and we bought enough nails to keep us busy during that day, and then we'd wait till the next mornin' to do the same. But," he said, and his face was long that evening, "windows and doors are big and come to a lot of money, and we just can't buy those."

I said, "You can make doors."

"Yes," he said, "but the two outside doors on that two-room schoolhouse are store-boughten doors, and it'd look funny to have the third room with a homemade door."

Then I said, "Yes, but there's an inside door between those two rooms—it's a store-boughten door too. Take it and put it on the outside of the new room, and then build you an inside door to put where it was. Then all the outside doors will be store-boughten."

"Now that's an idea," they said. "We'll do that. We hadn't

thought of it. But that don't help us none on the windows."

"I know it doesn't," I said, "and I'm sorry. But windows cost money and I can't buy them. I've promised all the money I can beg, and I don't dare go in any deeper."

After much discussion—and very discouraging discussion —I said to them, "Gentlemen, I've been raised to believe that after we have done everything we can for ourselves, we can then go to God and ask Him to do the rest. Now let's make this the subject of prayer and ask God to give us somehow or other the money for those windows so that we may be able to open school in the short time that we have left."

They said they didn't know, they'd never thought of praying for a thing like that; but if I said to do it, they would. And they went home, and I know they did.

After I had put my babies to bed that night, I went into the living room and found Dr. Sloop reading his American Medical Association *Journal*. I had told the story of the windows to him at the supper table. Just as I went in, he looked up.

"Here's the answer to your prayer," he said.

"What?"

"Here's a young man in Ohio who's had the same difficulty you have. And he used unbleached domestic to stretch over the window openings in place of sash. He found that it was very satisfactory, that the air that came through the domestic furnished ventilation—really better ventilation than they had when they opened the windows occasionally when the stoves made the room too hot. He found also that it took less coal to keep an even temperature such as he wanted, and he had a thermometer in his school room. So," Doctor said, "now there's your chance."

And I said, "I saw some in the store down in the village for five cents a yard." Those were the good old days! "I'm going to go down there and get it, if we can just figure how much

I need." So we calculated how much cloth it would take to cover those windows.

After a while he said to me, "I'm afraid this is a false hope. The children will cut those cloth windows to ribbons."

"No, they won't!" I said. "These children are so interested in getting a better education and having a better schoolhouse that they won't mutilate a thing."

"Well," he said, "the dogs will jump through them."

"I hadn't thought about that," I said. "But we can take the top sashes out of the windows in the two-room schoolhouse—as far as we need them—and put them in the bottom parts of the new windows, and then finish the top sections of all the windows with unbleached domestic. Now let us get a measure as closely as we can of what we'll need."

We began figuring the number of yards that would be needed to do the top sections. When we finished, I said, "Now five times that many yards means so much money." I named the amount. "And now"—I held out my hand—"please give it to me."

"Well," Doctor said, "I didn't bargain for that."

I said, "I can't help it. This isn't any bargain; these are facts. Let's pay for that cloth, and tomorrow I'll take it to those men."

Ungrudgingly, Doctor gave me the money. The next morning I went to the store, bought the cloth, and carried it to the men. I explained how it should be put up and how I had found out about its use that way. I told them I thought the whole thing was a mighty good lesson to us in what we called answer to prayer. And I don't believe any more effective lesson was ever taught in that community.

We used those unbleached-domestic windows for five years. And not a child or a dog harmed them.

## 13

WE hadn't been long settled in the mountains before we found ourselves face to face with what we considered one of the most tragic facts of mountain life, the widely accepted practice of children marrying at the very beginning of their adolescent years.

Frequently girls married at thirteen; they considered themselves old maids if they were not married at fifteen or sixteen. And if a boy hadn't married at sixteen or seventeen, his fellows would begin to poke fun at him and charge him with being "a poor hand with the wimmenfolks." A boy who had reached voting age without being married was a rarity indeed; he was headed toward permanent bachelorhood, everyone agreed.

So it was not so unusual to see children fourteen and fifteen years old, little girls hardly out of their pigtails, married to boys of sixteen and seventeen who tried desperately to demonstrate their masculinity by growing mustaches and even sideburns and beards in some cases.

Young boys in those days left the home nest early. Frequently they would go off to "public work," as it was called. That meant that they got employment at sawmills or even went into the northwest to do logging, or obtained jobs in the mines. All a fellow had to have to be considered a first-class matrimonial catch was a cow, an acre of ground, and a little cabin on it. He was then a man on his own and ready to get married. It mattered not that the cow was poor, the acre of ground hilly and filled with stumps, and the cabin a one-room shack; he was ready to start raising a family.

Often we felt like weeping. It seemed so unfair to these children; they were being deprived of their childhood, they were being thrust abruptly from babyhood into the respon-

Then and Now:
(*right*) Crossnore's
first one-room
schoolhouse;
(*below*) the high
school today, one
of the twenty-five
school buildings.

The two Doctors Sloop underneath their "antiseptic" apple tree which was for years one of the safest places to operate in Crossnore.

sibilities of an adult. Many little girls were nursing babies long before they would in the normal course of things have given up playing with baby dolls. The death toll of infants was high, and many little girl wives died in childbirth, while others grew old with childbearing at twenty-five or thirty.

We saw many such cases, and it grieved us. We knew that the children would never get far in their schooling if they were bent on getting married in their middle teens. We talked against it whenever and wherever we had the opportunity, but we realized that we were rowing upstream with a straw for a paddle.

One day, though, we came right up against this problem and saw it starkly outlined. We had never had it come so close home. And this is how it came about.

We had discovered a very interesting family living near us and had taken a decided liking to each member. It was our interest in this family, inspired by the bravery of the father and his motherless children in their efforts to keep the pathetic little group together, along with my growing alarm at the prevalence of child marriages in our mountain communities, that led me to make an investment that has paid marvelous dividends in the succeeding years.

The mother had died when the oldest girl was ten. There were four or five younger children, and one was barely learning to walk. The ten-year-old sister had taken over the management of the home, because the father's work was at a sawmill which moved from place to place and sometimes was a good distance from his home. But he was a faithful father, and every Wednesday night he came home to see how the children were getting along, and again on Saturday nights— folks worked on Saturdays in those days—so that he would be home Sunday, for he was superintendent of the Sunday school.

The little girl's name was Hepsy. When Hepsy was twelve, two years after her mother's death, the baby died of scarlet fever; the other children survived it. Two or three of them were still quite young, and the burden upon the child was very heavy.

Now, I had offered sewing lessons to a group of girls in the community, and they organized a class that came to my house every Thursday afternoon. Hepsy was one of them. Always she was there—with the two youngest children. She usually walked the long way from home. She would put the two tots down on the floor, with some little thing to play with —I would find them some toys—and they would play while the class went on.

One cold winter afternoon when the ground was covered with a deep snow, I wondered if the girls would brave the weather to come to the sewing class. I sat looking out the window, and after a while I saw them plodding along through the snow—all of them except Hepsy. When they had put up their wraps and got settled, I inquired about Hepsy. Why hadn't she come? She was always so faithful. I wondered what the trouble was. Were the children sick?

"No'm, ain't none of them sick, Mis' Sloops," one of the girls ventured to reply, "leastways we ain't heard nothin' about it if they are. But I don't think Hepsy's acomin' to the class any more."

"But why?" I asked, amazed.

"Hepsy's agoin' to git married," the girl answered, "and they's amovin' t'other side o' the ridge."

"Get married! But Hepsy's only twelve years old!"

I knew that the law would not permit a person to marry under fourteen. That was the North Carolina law. Now one must be sixteen, I'm glad to say, and eighteen without the consent of the parents. But then it was fourteen.

"Yes'm," the girl said. "But Hepsy'll soon be thirteen, and as soon as you're turned thirteen you're agoin' into fourteen and can git married." The girl grinned. "Hepsy's been

70

acourtin' and as soon as she's turned thirteen she's agoin' to git married, they do say."

I was sick. The man they told me she was planning to marry, I knew, was more than twice her age and a drunkard and moonshiner. Hepsy was such a promising child, by all means the brightest one in my little sewing class. Her experience in mothering the family had made a real woman of her at that early age. She had a sense of responsibility that was remarkable. She might make a mark in the world. And now she was about to throw away every chance by marrying this no-good. It nearly broke my heart.

After the girls had gone I thought and thought, and I prayed over it. And a few days later, when I learned that Hepsy's father was at home, I went to see him.

"Hepsy is a smart child," I said to him. "She's taken all the schooling we can give her here at the present time. So I've decided she ought to go off to school, and I'm going to see to it that she gets to go."

The father protested at first. He said he'd have nobody to look after the other children.

"But if you let Hepsy get married and move away, you'll not have her anyway," I argued. "Anyhow, you ought to let this child have a chance. She deserves it." I talked and talked, something I've never had trouble doing.

I won out. He agreed to let her go to Banner Elk, some thirty miles away, where they had a good preparatory school. The next oldest girl was now as old as Hepsy had been when her mother died, and the father thought she would be able to care for the children, especially now that the baby was dead. And he was pleased that Hepsy was going to get an education. Once he had been ambitious himself, but he had never had an opportunity to satisfy his ambition. But of course he had no money to give Hepsy. It took every cent he could make to provide a very modest living for the family.

71

It was up to me to get Hepsy off to school and keep her there. How would I do it?

The first thing I did was to write to some of my friends at Davidson and ask them if they wouldn't make contributions toward helping pay Hepsy's expenses at Banner Elk that year. And they did. They were most generous.

But what about clothes that would permit her to be presentable? I didn't have the money to buy cloth to make clothes for the child. How was she going to get them? I had promised to get her off to school for the term starting after Christmas, and that wasn't many weeks away.

I remembered two cousins of mine, sisters, who were small women about Hepsy's size. So I wrote to them and asked them if they would send me some of their old clothes. In my girlhood I had known these women and they had worn pretty clothes, and I just imagined Hepsy dressed up in their nice things.

Soon I had a letter from them. Yes, they were glad to help Hepsy, and they were sending the clothes in a trunk so that Hepsy might have it to take off to school with her.

I waited impatiently. Then one afternoon I looked out and saw the mica wagon coming in from down the country at the mines. It was hauling mica to the mica mill just beyond. Tied on the top of the wagon I saw the little trunk, bobbing around as the wagon rattled over the rough road. I could hardly wait for it to reach the house and for them to put the trunk down on the front porch. When they had put it down, I rushed in and got the key which had been sent to me by the two sisters. Then I ran back out to the porch, opened the trunk, lifted the lid.

And every dress was black!

The cousins had apparently been in mourning, and had done it thoroughly.

I took out black dress after black dress, and finally lifted out a bonnet with a crepe veil on it. My heart broke. The tears came. I put my head down on top of the little trunk.

An old woman came up unnoticed and saw me. Directly she touched my shoulder and inquired, her voice warm with sympathy, "Mis' Sloops, what's the matter? Is yo' folks dead?"

"No," I said, "but somebody else's are." Then I explained.

This woman had been one as interested as I in Hepsy's going off to school. She thought it was so fine for Hepsy to have a chance, and maybe other girls would get it too. She thought a moment. Then she spoke up.

"I wish them dresses was big enough for me," she said. "I'd shore buy one of them and that would help a little bit."

Then the idea came!

I took out armloads of those black dresses and hung them on the front porch. The neighbors saw them and the word went around. And they came and bought, and bought, and bought.

Suddenly the whole valley was in mourning!

How proud those women were of those well-made dresses. So they began to beg me to get more.

Doctor said that as he would ride up the valley on horseback going to see a patient and maybe in a great hurry, some woman would come out and flag him down and say, not "Has my baby got the croup, you reckon?" as he thought she would, but "Doctor, when's Mis' Sloops agoin' to git some more o' them black dresses? I want one so bad."

So Doctor told me to write for some more dresses, and to be sure they sent black ones. I did write to my friends for more dresses, but I didn't say they must be black, though I did tell them that "black was preferred at the present time."

The dresses began coming in. I sold them at the house. My mountain friend sold them from her front porch. We took in the money for Hepsy's going-off-to-school clothes.

The gingham was bought, the hair ribbons were bought, the pretty underclothes were made, and soon everything was ready for Hepsy to go off to school. And her dresses were just like other dresses that came from the low country where they had big stores and where they knew what it was to be stylish.

Out of that strange but wonderful experience came the old-clothes sales. And out of the old-clothes sales much of Crossnore was built. Old clothes, old shoes, old hats grew into buildings of frame and brick and concrete blocks. Old clothes turned into training, education, a better way of life for children, scores and hundreds of bright mountain children, who were shortly to become leaders in the movement to establish a happier manner of living for the people of our mountain region.

But not immediately, of course. For a time we continued our front-porch sales. We got Hepsy off to Banner Elk after Christmas. She liked the school. We had prevented another child marriage, and I was thankful for that.

And then, before her first term was half over, other girls came to me and begged for help so they could go off to school. I promised. I always undertook far more than it appeared at the time that I could accomplish. And somehow, thanks to a kind Providence, things almost always panned out.

Having stumbled into this valuable source of income, we began to press the old-clothes sales and to save every penny we could produce through them. We decided to have regular sales days—Saturdays, at first—and to hang the clothes out in the yard on a clothes line and let the people come and buy them. By displaying them more effectively and spreading the word about, we would be able to sell them to better advantage, we felt.

From that, the present sales store developed.

But not that quickly. The next step was to put up a chicken-wire fence around a spot of ground on which we could hold our sales after we had prepared the clothes for selling. And the people came, often long before breakfast.

We had been fortunate in obtaining two of our best-liked

people in the community to take charge of the sales. Uncle Gilmer Johnson had a handlebar mustache (it has since turned white) which seemed to stamp him as a storekeeper, and a manner that fitted him for the job of dealing with his mountain neighbors. Aunt Pop, his wife—her name must have been Poppy but everybody in that country called her Aunt Pop, and few perhaps had ever stopped to wonder if she could have had another name—was a perfect counterpart for Uncle Gilmer. She was small, blond, wiry, and as energetic as a cricket. Her blue eyes twinkled, and she was always smiling. She had a heavy head of hair rolled into a tight knot in the back that seemed nicely to balance off Uncle Gilmer's huge mustache. She is gone now, but nobody at Crossnore and for miles around will ever forget Aunt Pop.

One day Uncle Gilmer told me that at one o'clock that morning some folks came to his house and waked him up. "Uncle Gilmer, it's Sat'day now," they said; "git up and sell us some clothes." They were camping nearby; they had decided to try to get a first chance at the clothes.

That led Uncle Gilmer to urge me to set a definite time for the opening, and we set ten o'clock, so that the people from a distance could be there when we started selling and have an equal chance with those who lived nearby.

The chicken-wire fence worked very well for a while. The people could see what was happening. Uncle Gilmer and Aunt Pop and others in his family would come by from their little warehouse in the yard—which had been their feed house, I believe—and put the clothes on some rude tables that had been made inside the wire enclosure. The people would stand there and watch for what they wanted most, and when the gate was opened there was a football rush and each would run to the table which he thought most likely to have the things he wanted.

They would sit on top of the tables, on the clothes. We begged them not to do the hats that way, but that was the

75

only way a fellow could be sure of keeping what he wanted; others were coming along and grabbing. He would sit there until he got out from under himself the pieces he wanted; then he would take them to Uncle Gilmer to have them priced.

They tell the story—I can't vouch for the truth of it, but it's a good story anyway—of an old man who always wore a swallow-tailed coat and invariably was one of the first on hand at sales days. In fact, the story is that he got a dry-goods box and set it beside the fence. Then, just as the gate was opened at ten o'clock, he'd get on the box and jump over the fence, race to the table containing some item he had spotted and squat down on it until he had the chance of taking it to Uncle Gilmer and paying for it.

One day, as he was sitting on the box waiting, some mischievous boys slipped up and tacked his long coattails to the box. The gate was opened a moment later. The old fellow gave a leap to sail over the fence, and jerked off his coattails!

But soon we had to abandon that chicken-wire-fence arrangement and move into a building. We have built one store after another through the years until we now have a nice, up-to-date sales store—with the same names across the front, AUNT POP'S AND UNCLE GILMER'S STORE. Without the money that comes from the sale of old clothes, we'd have a hard time financing Crossnore.

One of the great advantages to the people was, and still is, the barter plan. People had been buying for cash only. It was the only thing we could do. And cash was awfully scarce. It was during the depression that one man came and said, "Mr. Gilmer, I want this suit so bad. I'd give Mis' Sloops six hundred pounds of cabbage for this suit, but I can't pay money for it." Uncle Gilmer told me. We worked out a deal. And that was the beginning of our barter plan.

The barter works well for Crossnore school and for the people. We sell them clothes they want, and they sell us their produce. When we buy a load of cabbage or beans or corn, we give the seller coupons good for purchase of articles at the store. And we give them more in coupons than we would in cash, so that at the store they can get more clothes, since the price is the same whether they pay cash or coupons. And since the clothes cost us nothing, we can afford to be more generous with the coupons. It's a good plan.

## 14

WHILE I was busy during these first few years in Crossnore at the tasks of helping Doctor practice medicine, getting in some good licks for the improvement of both the school facilities and the quality of the teaching, aiding in the Sunday school and the work of the church, selling old clothes to help Hepsy and other children get off to school, and doing countless other things that defy cataloguing, Doctor had got himself warmly interested in still another project.

When we came to the mountains to live there were of course no electric lights. We had kerosene lamps and lanterns. Doctor generally carried a lantern when he answered calls. Often that lantern served well, for sometimes when he got to a mountain home high in the hills the kerosene had given out and there was only firelight. I had known him to do operations—and sometimes major operations—by the light of his lantern.

So after we had come over to Crossnore and begun to get ourselves established, one of the first things that Doctor wanted to do was to get electric power in our home so that we could have electric lights.

He ordered catalogues and he pored over books on electricity. But the cost was so high—the cost of these independent home systems, like one called Delco, for instance. We just didn't have that kind of money.

But Doctor wasn't to be stopped. He decided he would build his own plant. He had bought a piece of property down on the river at a place where two steep hills came right down to the water, and the little stream was very narrow there. He saw right off that this would be a fine place to build his dam.

There were trees on that tract, too, very large trees. He hired a man to help him and they cut down trees and built a log dam, using cement to chink the cracks in the logs. And it was a good dam.

But a dam would be no good without a dynamo to make the power. So Doctor set his mind to getting a dynamo. He remembered that while he was a student at Davidson College he had seen two old dynamos that had been set aside when the college changed over to the Southern Power Company, which later became the Duke Power Company.

He wrote to the president of the college, Dr. William J. Martin, who was my brother, that he wanted to buy one of those dynamos. The president wrote back that the dynamos were being sold for junk. They were being offered for fifty dollars apiece but had not been bought. He said that they had been tested, because Dr. Vardell had wanted one for Flora Macdonald College if he could use it. The electricians told him it couldn't be used, however, because it was out of date and out of repair and parts were not to be gotten. So my brother said that Dr. Sloop shouldn't waste fifty dollars on that dynamo.

I wrote to my brother then and told him that Doctor had a right to waste fifty dollars on that dynamo if he wanted to, that if he was in a city he'd spend that much on pleasure, and to let him get that dynamo and play with it. So my brother agreed.

Doctor refused to let it go to Charlotte for repair, but insisted on having it sent to Crossnore.

That dynamo weighed 2300 pounds and required four horses to pull the wagon to haul it the 15 miles from the railroad over rough, steep mountain roads, muddy as could be. And it took a day to get the horses and wagon down to the railroad station and a day to get them back.

Late in the afternoon I was at work unpacking clothes for the sale the next day, and Aunt Pop and Uncle Gilmer were working with me. The driver came down and said, "I've got that great big thing up yonder on the road. I'll have to take out two of my horses and bring it down the hill to your house. But I don't know what we are agoin' to do with it then."

"Oh, Doctor's not here, and I don't know when he's coming," I said, "but we'll see what we can do—Uncle Gilmer and I; Aunt Pop can finish with the clothes."

So Uncle Gilmer and I went up the hill to the house. He was intensely interested in the dynamo, because it was something new. We suggested that the man take his two front horses out and back down the hill to our house. It wasn't a very steep hill, and the road was pretty straight.

So he did that. The house at that place, being on the side of a hill, was more than six feet above the ground. Under there Doctor had a number of short logs, 2½ or 3 feet long, cut out of big trees to be split up for wood. We decided that we would roll four of those together near the edge of the house, back the thing as nearly against it as possible, and slide it down some thick timbers that we had there. With a crowbar to make it move, we pushed it to the back of the wagon, and we said our prayers when we started it sliding down.

It wasn't a very steep slide, because the logs were nearly as high as the wagon bed. But it went on down and it didn't break anything. Oh, how I did pray that it would have a successful landing!

And it did. The men had been very much interested in what they were doing and had been most careful. There was danger of breaking the wagon, there was danger of the horses' jerking and jumping. So we had taken them out of

79

harness. We had tried to guard against trouble. And it had worked out.

When Doctor came home a little later I said to him, "Your baby's down under the house."

"What do you mean?" he said.

I said, "That thing you had brought up from Davidson. And it weighs twenty-three hundred pounds."

"Oh, has it come!" he said, and his eyes just shone. "Where is it? Where's the wagon?"

"The wagon's gone on home," I said.

"Well, how in the world did you get it off the wagon?" he asked, his eyes incredulous.

"I didn't do it," I said. "Charlie and Uncle Gilmer did it." I laughed. "But I bossed it."

He grinned, and went on downstairs. He came back up— I was getting supper—and passed through the kitchen a time or two. I saw him go by with some sheet copper in his hands, and then with some tin cans. I, of course, don't know to this day what he did, for I'm not mechanical. But he went down there and worked with it.

He came back up directly and said to me, "Don't you want to see it"—he called it by a pet name, "Lizzie," I believe— "don't you want to see it run?"

"Run?" I said.

"Yes," he replied.

"But Brother said it had to go to a shop to be repaired."

"It has," he said, grinning. "I've repaired it."

It was running! He had a battery, I suppose, attached to it so that one part was running—not the whole thing—but he had fixed the part that had needed repairing. Anyway, he had proved that it was workable.

They hauled that dynamo over to the dam, and it was a terrible job doing it, but the horses made it. They put it in the little powerhouse that Doctor had built for it. Then there was the job of running wire from the powerhouse out to our

80

house, which was a mile away. We didn't have money to pay workmen to do that.

But Doctor got his poles and placed them along the way the line was to run. Will then was still a baby, possibly toddling, but not older than that, and so Doctor had no one in the family to help him with those poles. But some neighbors did, and he got his poles up and everything ready for the wire.

Then he said to me, "Now I'm going to buy a wire stretcher, because I'll be needing one all the time, and you and I will stretch that wire."

I said, "All right." I didn't really know what he was talking about.

So we would go out with our tools and things, and I'd take the baby and set him against a stump—so that he wouldn't roll down hill—and give him some playthings to play with right in front of him, and then I'd do the ground work and Doctor would do the work up on the poles. So that's the way we stretched the wire, and finally the job was complete.

Already Doctor had wired our house, and now the current had been brought to it. He told Emma, who then was five years old, to watch and see what was going to happen. Now, he told her, the bulbs he had put up were going to shine. She had been very interested in those bulbs, but they hadn't been shining. Now they would, her daddy told her.

I remember her squeal when the lights flashed on!

From that time on I felt, like I told somebody, that every time I turned those lights on, somebody had given me a Christmas present.

People came to see them. "They say that if you punch a place in your wall the light will burn," they said. "We want to see it."

Not long after that, our neighbor, Mr. Brown, came over. He lived about a half mile away. He said, "Me and my boys will put up the line between your house and mine if you'll sell me the electricity and wire our house."

"All right," Doctor told him, "we'll try it."

So they set up the poles and strung the wire, and Doctor wired their house. And before long the Browns had electricity.

"Now if you can do it for Mr. Brown, you can do it for me," I told Doctor. "I want electricity at the school."

So he decided to put some lights in at the school. And it did work. But that was about all the load his plant would carry.

Then we had to begin to think about ways of spreading electricity around the valley. Doctor explained that in order to get more current for new requirements he'd have to change from direct to alternating current. "And I can't afford to buy an alternating current dynamo." Then I saw that twinkle in his eyes. "But I believe I can fix the dynamo we have."

He sent off and bought a little book on electricity. He had had physics at college—all they would teach—and so he was fairly familiar with the subject. This little book had a red-leather binding, and it was small enough to go into his pocket. As he would ride along on horseback going to visit his patients, he would read the little book and get himself educated on electricity.

Uncle Bob Franklin sent for him one day. He and his wife had no children; they were a very devoted old couple that we respected highly. Uncle Bob sent word that his wife was very sick and he wanted Doctor to come right away.

So Doctor put his little red book in his pocket as usual and mounted his horse and went on down the road. As he went he was reading. When he neared the old gentleman's home, Uncle Bob came running out to meet him.

"Doctor," he said, "I'm so glad to see you. And it does a man so much good to send for a doctor and see him comin' readin' his Bible."

"Now, Doctor," I said that night when he told me about it, "you know you didn't spoil that for Uncle Bob; you know you didn't tell him you weren't reading your Bible."

"I certainly did," Doctor said. "And I got Uncle Bob so interested in that book he was almost ready to read it himself."

Uncle Bob's wife got well even though it wasn't the Bible.

People kept coming to us to beg Doctor to put electricity into their houses. So Doctor decided he would rewind that dynamo so that it would produce alternating current. He needed some brass rings and a few other things that I don't remember about. He wrote to General Electric and asked them to sell him those things, and told them what he was going to do.

General Electric wrote back and said that they couldn't sell the rings, that it was a useless undertaking for him anyway, that there were a number of people who had thought that they could rewind a direct-current dynamo and make it work as an alternating-current dynamo, but that they just couldn't do it. But, they said, they would sell him an alternating-current one, and they sent him the price list.

"I don't care," Doctor said. "I know I can do it."

So he said one day to Uncle Alex, "I've ordered from Sears, Roebuck a little forge—a portable one—and we are going to make the rings for that alternating-current dynamo." Then he and Uncle Alex took some copper and some tin cans and went out to the dam.

And the rings were made. He brought some of them home to smooth them down with sandpaper, and Uncle Alex took the others home with him to smooth them down.

Then began the wiring. At first Doctor could wire them himself, but gradually that hole in the ring filled up and he couldn't do it any longer. There was one of the teachers, a very interesting young mountain woman and an excellent teacher, who used to go with him out to the dam to turn on the lights, and then when he was away she would go there to turn them on. So he said to her, "You'll have to come and wind this wire in the ring for me, because my hand is too big to go in it."

And she did. But it soon filled up so her hand wouldn't go in it. So she said, "Jean Elliott has a much smaller hand than I have, Doctor. I'll bring her out tomorrow afternoon, and we'll wire then."

Jean came and helped, but it filled up so her hand couldn't get in either. That night at supper Doctor said to Emma, who was now six, "Sister, you'll have to go and help Daddy wind that dynamo."

Her eyes shone. She'd love to. She had gone to the dam often with her father.

He said to me as they went out, "Well, we may finish the work before night. I'll take the boy with me."

"Now don't be late," I said. "I'll be awfully uneasy about the child out there."

"Oh, no," he said, "I'll be careful. I'll keep him in the power-house; I won't let him run around outside." He couldn't run much anyway on that rough ground, but I was afraid he'd fall and maybe roll into the river.

The afternoon wore on, and I had to get supper. I was there alone. And it began to get dark, and still they hadn't come. It got still darker, and I couldn't stand it any longer. So I lighted my lantern and started out along that dark trail. I made it all right until I got to Mill Timber Creek. The bridge over Mill Timber Creek—it was just a big log 30 feet long—was high up to prevent its being washed away by freshets. You had to go up a chicken walk, which was a board with strips across it, and go across the log and then down another chicken walk.

Doctor didn't mind that, and neither did the children. But I did. They had never put a handrail to it, and I didn't like to cross it. I wasn't supposed to anyway, they said.

84

But this night I knew I had to go across on that log. And when I got to the top of the chicken walk with the lantern in my hand, I didn't know what I was going to do. Finally, I started out a step or two, and I knew that wasn't going to do. I knew that when I got out over the water I'd get dizzy and fall. So I got down on my hands and knees and went a part of the way over, with the lantern hanging on my wrist.

Then I began to get dizzy. So I just straddled it and went across, hunching myself along until I got to the other side and thankful that it was dark and there was nobody around! Then I crawled down the chicken walk and started toward the dam.

When I came in sight of the powerhouse I saw the light burning inside and I felt better. After a while I got there and scrambled down the steep bank. I could hear them talking inside. I heard Emma, and she was crying.

"But, Daddy, Mama will be so scared if we don't go on home," she was whimpering.

"But, Sis," I heard Doctor say to her, "I'm just about through. I just want to finish this one little bit."

"But I don't think we ought to scare Mama so bad," Emma said.

Just then I knocked on the door.

"Come in," Doctor said.

I walked in. "Here's part of my family," I said, looking around. "But where's my baby?"

"He's over there in a box," Doctor said, "on a bundle of rags that I use to clean the dynamo."

When I picked up my baby, he was as black as he could be. He had smeared himself with those black, greasy rags and he looked perfectly awful, but he was sleeping just as soundly as if he were on a feather bed.

The next day the electric lights were turned on. Doctor's converted dynamo was working!

## 15

AS I look back almost forty years to those early days in the mountains, I realize that we too were pioneers. Life was often hard and sometimes the job of making a simple living was almost beyond accomplishment.

I wonder sometimes if the young people in the mountains today—or anywhere else—would come through as their grandparents did, and even their parents, were they suddenly to find themselves living in a world comparable to the world around Crossnore twoscore years ago. What would they do were they to find themselves without electric lights and power, without warm houses in the wintertime, without central heating, without electric stoves, bottled gas, radios, television sets, without automobiles—yes, and even without roads? They would rise to meet the situation, I'm sure they would. But it would be tough.

And it was tough then.

It was tough riding horseback far into the lonely hills to visit some sick man or woman or little child, someone sawed half in two in a dreadful sawmill accident or shot in a brawl over the division of a run of moonshine liquor, or ill of typhoid fever or suffering terribly from a strangulated hernia. It was hard work and cold, and often we came home from it worn out and discouraged.

It was rewarding too, though never in a financial way. But we hadn't come to the mountains to get rich through the accumulation of money. And few were the mornings after a day and night of grueling toil and testing that we did not arise eager to face another day's challenge.

Being pioneers, we were often forced to improvise, just as Doctor did in building his own power plant and converting an old dynamo to his needs. Frequently we did that in

86

our medical work. We improvised operating rooms for instance. Often out under the shade of a large tree we would set up our operating table, borrowed usually from the patient's kitchen or made from several boards laid across two wooden horses. We improvised instruments, Doctor figured out new techniques. I remember many a time how I pictured in my mind's eye, as I helped him with an operation, Doctor bending over a patient in some great hospital's white operating room, in Boston or Philadelphia or New York, as he performed with skillful hands a delicate operation that saved the life of his patient.

Nor was there anything wrong with that picture, except that the white operating room was the great outdoors and the assisting surgeons and nurses were a handful of the patient's anxious relatives and friends and Doctor's country-doctor wife. For Doctor was the same in both pictures. His operations did save many lives, and I happily join countless ones in the mountains who call him great and bless him for what he has done and for the manner of his doing it.

Those early years were so filled with living. Doctor was always doing things, and I was always talking of what I'd like to do—and sometimes doing it. For there was so much to be done. And after forty years there still is.

For instance, we had hardly moved the old school building and put up the two-room structure, and then added the third room, before we were beginning to be overrun with children. And immediately we were faced with the problem of improvising.

And that always brings to my mind one of the boys we had met in our short stay at Plumtree before moving to Cross-nore. After all these years I can close my eyes and see him clearly. He had a heavy black beard; I don't think he'd ever shaved at all.

This boy told us that he had been raised in Virginia, that his father had seventeen sons and two daughters. He said that up in those mountains they did nothing but make liquor, and in fact his brothers and his father had a still. He came in contact with a minister who had been a Davidson College student and was a friend of ours. The boy was converted, and he made up his mind that he was going to get an education; he couldn't read or write, and he didn't learn to until he was twenty-seven years old.

The minister suggested that he come down to Plumtree, and the minister wrote us about him.

Joe was a wonderful fellow, full of energy and determined to learn. He was head of the school's kitchen force, and I have heard him so often when the things were cooking as he read aloud to himself in his effort to learn to read. And that boy never gave up in his determination to have an education.

When we came to Crossnore he followed us a little later, and we found that he wasn't well. We thought that he should lead an outdoor life. He had no definite signs of tuberculosis, but it looked mighty like it. So we undertook to put him to sleeping outdoors.

We got him a job that was outdoors—riding the mail. He finished high school and was ready to go to college. Just before he was to leave for Davidson we received in the second-hand-clothes sale a tent. It was a joy to us, because now Joe could sleep outdoors.

He took that tent with him and spent his freshman year at Davidson sleeping in it in the yard of one of our friends. He became popular at once. He no longer wore his beard. But he did carry with him as a pet a big rattlesnake which he had caught on Doctor's property here. He had pulled out the rattler's fangs and so he was harmless. Joe fixed him a home in a barrel and the boys all came to see the snake and the boy who slept in a tent.

He grew steadily stronger, finished his course there, and went on into the ministry to become a wonderfully useful minister.

Joe wasn't the only grown man who came to Crossnore as a pupil, I might point out. We have had a number of boys, and several girls, who were old enough to vote when they entered our school. The oldest was thirty-eight when he was graduated. I'd like to tell about him. He has been one of our important men at the school.

He had been married when a mere boy, one of those sixteen- or seventeen-year-old youngsters I have spoken about. He told me he just had to get married at that age, because another fellow was about to get his girl and he couldn't stand for that to happen. So he took no chances, and he married her while they were both children. And he had seven children before he decided to come to Crossnore to school! He declared he was going to stay in school, too, until he had earned his high-school diploma.

I told him that if he'd come to Crossnore to school, he could be a janitor and thus help to earn his keep. He came, and he brought four of the children with him. They helped him with the janitor work, and the five of them slept in one of the schoolrooms. It was sort of makeshift living, but they got along, and after a while he got that high-school diploma.

Then he went one year to Appalachian State Teachers' College at Boone, but he wasn't able to go on through without stopping. He skipped a year and worked. The next year he went back to Boone; and by that time his daughter was ready for college, and father and daughter were college students together.

He was persistent, determined to get a college education. And he got it, though it took him a long time. He would work and then go to school a while, and stop and work some more, and he'd go to summer school when he could. And finally he won his college diploma—at fifty-six!

He has been teaching at Crossnore since, and he's one of our best!

But I want to get back to Joe, that boy who had spent his

89

college years at Davidson living in a tent while he fought off tuberculosis.

That tent still belonged to us. So he sent it back. And just about that time we were in dire need of another schoolroom, and we just couldn't build it. We had already completed that third room onto our little two-room schoolhouse, and could not go ahead and build another one. The carpenters had to work for themselves awhile.

So we brought out the tent. When the opening day of school proved that we had more children than could be housed in the three-room schoolhouse, we put some in the tent. That was used throughout the winter.

Yes, it was cold, awfully cold, especially for those students who had to sit near the edge of the tent. We put a wooden floor down a couple of feet above the ground and then built up a wall about thirty inches high all around that. To the wall we fastened the tent. In the middle of the floor we put a stove, and the stovepipe went out, properly protected, through the top of the tent.

The teacher was the one who suffered most because she was the only one who had to stay there all the time; we changed the classes occasionally during the day and gave the students a chance to warm up. Among those who got in earliest there was a terrible rush to get nearest the stove.

And we did have some bitter weather that winter! There are some who remember to this day their experiences in learning arithmetic and history in that tent in nearly zero weather.

But the tent was only a temporary help. The children continued to swarm into our growing school. The only thing to do was to add two more rooms to the schoolhouse, and do it in a hurry. I had a little more money then, and so I could do things faster. We put up the outside walls of those two extra rooms, and put the roof on and the floor down. We had no money for partitions, and none for windows. Again our window sash was unbleached domestic; the partitions were building paper. But we taught a good school that fall, and gradually we put up partitions as patrons of the school gave us lumber.

So now we had five rooms, and they were full. We were teaching all the elementary grades by that time. And then we began more earnestly to talk of high school.

We had built in the meantime a little building on a swampy piece of land that was given us and that we drained with free labor. But we had trouble getting roofing. Roofing was such an expensive part of the building that nobody could give that to us. So we built two rooms, one on top of the other, a very small two-story building that required a roof for but one room. The children laughed and called the little structure Treasure Island, for they had reached the point in their studies where they enjoyed that book. Upstairs in Treasure Island we taught home economics; downstairs we taught manual training.

The old schoolhouse that the oxen had pulled across the flat had been torn down—much to my distress—and used in building a new post office. They had done it while I was away from home.

Counting Treasure Island, we now had seven schoolrooms. A school near us, at Altamont, had children ready for high school but no school to attend. So we decided that we would start teaching first-year high school at Crossnore and let the Altamont children attend. The number ready for that training was small, but even then the only place we had to put them was in a little lean-to on the back of the shop, which I called the Wart, because it was so out of place.

The Wart was about eight feet wide and twelve feet long. It had no windows in it whatsoever, but having learned about unbleached domestic, we cut a piece out of the side of each of two walls and stretched the unbleached domestic over these openings, going the full length of 12 feet on one side and 8 on the other.

We put into that room some homemade desks and left a little aisle to walk in.

That was our first year of high school at Crossnore.

Most of those boys and girls who went to school in that little room not only were graduated from high school but later were graduated from college. Unless my memory is playing tricks on me, I think there were sixteen students that first year—sixteen in that little room. They must have been sitting in each other's laps.

We'll never forget the Wart.

# 16

EDUCATION was on the move at Crossnore, though we were still down in that little circular flat. But soon we would begin to move up the rise.

Luckily, we were ready. We had the land.

One day, some time before, Uncle Elias came to see me. He told me he needed a little money.

"I want to sell you some land," he added. "I got to fee my lawyer. I'll let you have the land right. I'll sell you seventeen acres of it for thirty-five dollars an acre."

"But I haven't got that kind of money, Uncle Elias," I told him.

"You got some," he said, "and I won't need it all right now. I just want enough now to fee my lawyer."

I wanted that land. I counted my money. All I could raise was $102.

"That's enough," he said. "You can give me a note for the rest. I'll wait."

The whole amount came to $595. I paid him the $102 and gave him the note for the remainder.

Pretty soon the story began to get around that I had paid

Uncle Elias the tremendous price of thirty-five dollars an acre for that rocky hillside. Some of my neighbors were outraged.

"He beat you to death," they said. "That there land won't raise an acre of corn all put together."

"But I don't aim to raise corn on it," I said. "I want to raise a hundred children on it." I already knew what I hoped to do.

Some days after that Uncle Will Franklin came along in his wagon. He was one of our great characters. Tall, lean, stoop-shouldered, he wore a thin chin beard. He walked with long slow strides and talked in a slow drawl to match his walking. He was known over that country as a good farmer who raised his own wheat, a fine housebuilder. One of his enterprises was operating a tannery. Uncle Alex Johnson would make Uncle Will's shoes in return for using Uncle Will's leather to make shoes for himself and the members of his family.

Uncle Will was riding up through the land I had bought from Uncle Elias. I sat on the tailpiece of the wagon as it went slowly up the hill.

"Just look at all that land to put houses on, Uncle Will," I said, sweeping my arm in an arc to embrace my newly bought acres.

"Elias beat you to death," he said. "All put together it ain't worth $150. Me and Lum's done looked it over."

"I don't think Elias beat me," I said. "I'm satisfied."

Uncle Will shook his head. "You been beat good," he insisted.

I saw Lum Biggerstaff in another day or two. Lum had a sawmill and a small farm. Despite the fact that he had lost a hand in a sawmill accident, he was quite a craftsman and was known far and wide as a very fine coffinmaker.

"They tell me you been beat out," Lum said. "Ain't nothin' on that there land but rocks and Indian arrowheads. You

93

knowed it's been timbered by Ritter Lumber Company, didn't you?"

"Yes, but that was years ago. There's still good timber on that land, and besides, I want it for building houses on," I told him.

"Well, Elias give you a skinnin'," he declared. "I'm so ashamed of him for atakin' advantage of a woman that me and Will Franklin will set up a mill on it for you. You might get somethin' out of it, but Elias shore give you a beatin'."

They set up the sawmill, and Fred McKinney came and started cutting down the trees. He soon found he was getting so much cut that he put another team to hauling. Uncle Will began to fuss because there was so much lumber. When Fred had cut over the tract the lumber company sent a man up to estimate the lumber and he offered me two thousand dollars for it!

"I'm not going to sell," I told the man. "I'm going to build buildings with that lumber."

Shortly after that the J. Walter Wright Lumber Company, which did a tremendous lumber business in that area of the mountains, got the offer of a contract to provide a certain type of high-grade lumber for finishing boats. They sent a man over to look at my lumber and he found it was just the sort he needed. He would buy the whole lot, which wouldn't be enough for his needs, of course, but he wanted it. And he made me an offer—four thousand dollars!

Uncle Will heard about it. He shook his head. "You can't never keep up with a woman," he observed philosophically.

But I didn't sell. I had other ideas.

# 17

WE were making progress in education at Crossnore, we were moving up the slope, figuratively and actually, but there were still many problems to be solved, problems arising out of old customs and traditions as well as the general apathy of some of our parents.

One of the difficulties was that of grading the children. Many parents felt that their boys and girls should move up a grade each year; whether or not a child had completed the work required for promotion hardly entered into their thinking. In the old days there had been little effort at grading; the children had gone to school two months a year or four months or whatever the limited term provided, and at a certain age—often in the early teens—they had quit school. But now we were trying to standardize our schoolwork, and sometimes we ran into difficulties.

But an even greater problem was attendance, getting parents to send their children to school and send them regularly. Not all parents offended, of course, comparatively few, in fact, but some were real problems. We had a state compulsory-attendance law, but back in the coves and the hollows some parents paid little attention to it.

I had been appointed truant officer, and I was determined to see to it that all the children who were of school age should be in school. I remember one man—who must remain nameless—gave me a lot of trouble. This man had taken a little girl, some relative, I believe she was, whose parents had died, to rear. But he would keep her home from school any time the fancy struck him.

Several times I had seen him and talked with him about the importance of sending Roxie to school. I had warned him that I would have him arrested if he didn't reform his ways. He would promise to let the child come to school regularly, and then he'd keep her home.

So after a while I did have him arrested and carried before the magistrate. He was so mad he didn't know what to do. I had told him that the little girl was going to have a chance in life, that I was determined she would have, that I was going to have this child taken from him unless he did better by her.

He said, "You can have her and welcome. I don't want her," and got up and started out. The magistrate called him and said, "But wait. This is your second offense, and I'll have to fine you five dollars."

"I'll never pay it," he said.

The magistrate said, "Oh, yes, you will."

And while we were comforting the little girl, he persuaded the man to pay the fine. But he said, "I don't aim to keep the girl."

He went back home to get her clothes, he said, but she said she had next to nothing there. On the way, though, he partly repented and bought her a new pair of shoes and a dress and sent them back to me. We arranged a place for her to live, and we kept her in school.

Time went on, and the attendance improved. But they reported to me that Uncle Abe Calloway's son had stopped coming to school. Uncle Abe operated a gristmill in the community, and everyone knew him, because everyone sooner or later came to his mill. He was of medium-heavy build, dark hair, dark brown eyes—his physique somehow seemed to accentuate his stubbornness.

Uncle Abe was keeping his boy, now in his teens, at home to run the gristmill. There was no reason why Uncle Abe shouldn't run it himself, except that he preferred to talk to the neighbors (who brought their corn there to be ground) and have the boy run the mill. He said the boy had got big enough to do it, and he proposed to let him.

It wouldn't have done to let Uncle Abe continue to flout the law. That boy was in a public place. Everybody who came there saw him, and they knew he was of school age. If Uncle Abe was permitted to get by with it, then what would prevent others from disregarding the law?

I wrote him notes, and I sent people to see him. But old

Uncle Abe was obstinate; he would not send that boy to school. So then I had him arrested. It was an awful day, a raw November day. I had been in the magistrate's courtroom a good many times and had always found other women there. But when I went in to this courtroom this day, there wasn't a woman present. There were at least a dozen men from up on the creek where Uncle Abe lived, and I was told that these men were dangerous. The magistrate even wanted me to be careful how I dealt with them, and I promised I would.

We had the hearing. It was a long affair, and we argued with Uncle Abe and tried to make him agree to pay the fine the magistrate assessed against him and then give us his word he'd send the boy to school. But he just would not. His older son—the one who had paid the fine for refusing to send the little girl to school—also argued with him; told him to go ahead and pay it. But still Uncle Abe shook his head.

Then I said, "Well, I'm sorry, but you'll have to send him to jail, Mr. Johnson"—that was the magistrate—"and I expect he's never been to jail before."

"No, I ain't," said Uncle Abe. "I don't know what it looks like from the inside looking out, but I know what it looks like from the outside looking in."

So the magistrate sentenced him to go to jail. And then we called for the officer, who had been standing around there during the afternoon. But he had fled. So we had to deputize someone else to take Uncle Abe to the officer's house, which wasn't very far away.

After everybody had left, the young schoolteacher said to me, "Mrs. Sloop, I declare I'm sorry you had to do it. I'm actually scared to go home."

"Oh," I said, "hang around awhile. These men will disappear."

The men followed me out. I chatted with them a little and then went on, and I met Aunt Pop. She said, "They tell me

97

you put that old gray-haired man in jail this afternoon for not sending his boy to school."

"I certainly did," I said. "I haven't gotten him there yet, but he's on his way."

She said, "Ain't you ashamed to do a thing like that?"

I said, "No, ma'am. He's got to be made an example of."

"Well," she said, "I'd be scared if I was in your place."

"I'm not scared, Aunt Pop," I said. "You all are mistaken in your opinion of mountain men. Mountain men aren't going to do me any harm. There's a certain something in them that, drunk or sober, they can be trusted by a woman, if she's the right kind of woman, and I don't think you ought to doubt them. I don't, and I'm not a bit afraid of them."

"Are you going to walk all the way home by yourself?" she asked me.

I said, "I certainly am. And you can too; and you're not in any danger."

"Law, no," she said. "I wouldn't never have sent him to jail, and they know I wouldn't."

But I waited around until the new deputy had returned and said he had delivered Uncle Abe to the regular officer. I thought everything would go well. It was late in the afternoon when I got home, and I went to work getting supper.

The next morning I had to go down to a meeting of the teachers, and when I got in they all began to laugh at me. I said, "What's the matter?"

"Hunh," they said. "Your bird's flown."

I said, "What bird?"

They said, "Your jailbird."

"You don't mean Uncle Abe broke out of jail?" I said.

"No," they said, "he never went to it."

"Why?" I asked.

They said the officer decided he would keep Uncle Abe at his house that night and take him to jail the next morning, and when he got up the next morning Uncle Abe was gone.

I went to the telephone and called up the officer. "Where's Uncle Abe?" I asked him. I was very mad.

"I don't know, Mrs. Sloop," he said. "He's gone. He said something about goin' to Tennessee last night. But he's gone."

"You know you were to deliver that man to jail, and you're doing a very dangerous thing."

"But I—I just can't help it, Mrs. Sloop," he said. "I couldn't take that old man to jail last night. He was old, and he was cold, and he'd've had to ride horseback. And I just put him to bed. I just couldn't take him that six miles on horseback at night. And so I gave him his supper and put him to bed and told him we'd go in the mornin'. And when the mornin' come, he was gone."

I said, "Yes, but that's your fault and your responsibility."

"He said somethin' 'bout goin' to Tennessee," he told me.

"I don't care what he said," I answered him. "He's not in Tennessee. Uncle Abe's over yonder running that gristmill right now, or seeing that his boy's doing it. You're going over there and get Uncle Abe and put him in jail, and report to me that he's in jail. And you're going to do it now."

He said to me, "Mrs. Sloop, I—I declare, can't you ask the sheriff to do that? You don't know those folks over there on that creek. I'd like for you to ask the sheriff to do that."

I said, "No, I'm not going to ask the sheriff, but if you'll come up here and catch my horse—he's in the pasture, and I can't catch him—but if you'll come up here and saddle him, I'll go with you. I'll take you over there and help you to arrest him."

He said, "Would you, sure?"

"I certainly would," I said.

"I guess they'd laugh at me if I done that," he told me. "I guess I better go by myself."

I said, "Well, you better go, and you can get the sheriff if you want to. But you're going to put that man in jail."

"Are you sure he's over there?" he asked.

I said, "No, I don't know anything about it—whether he's over there or not. But I feel sure he is. And if you don't find him, you let me know and I'll help you."

Late that afternoon I got a message that Uncle Abe was in jail.

The days passed. He was to stay five days. When the fifth day was over, they couldn't discharge him, because the clerk of the court was the only one who could write the discharge, and the clerk of the court had gone off for the Sunday, and was not in the county. So they kept him until Monday.

On Monday I did my washing. The little girl had gone off with her father, and I took the baby, Will, and went out to hang up the clothes. It was down beside a hill. I sat the baby beside a stump and gave him some things to play with, so that if he tossed them aside they would roll back against him and the stump. Then I went down the hill a little farther to hang out my clothes.

I looked up, and to my horror I saw Uncle Abe coming down the hill. He scared me so bad I told the biggest lie I ever told in my life. There was my little baby between me and him. And Uncle Abe had in his hand a knife that looked to me to be a foot long. It wasn't, of course. He had been whittling, but I didn't think about that.

I caught his eye as he came down the hill looking at me, and I said, "Oh, Uncle Abe, I'm so glad to see you." And I went up the hill holding out my hand. Now you know that was a lie; I'd rather have seen anybody else on earth. But all I wanted was to get to the baby before he did—with that knife in his hand.

He sat down right near the baby, and he looked up and said, "Well, I sot it out."

I said, "I see you did, Uncle Abe, and I hope you're a better man."

"Well," he said, "I don't know 'bout that, but I come by to aks you to do a favor for me. I done a lot o' thinkin' durin' that time, and I just made up my mind that you was a just woman."

I could have hugged him, dirty and ugly as he was, but he was still sitting down at the foot of the tree. I had the baby in my arms by that time. He went on, "I want you to do me a favor."

"What's that, Uncle Abe?" I asked him.

"Well," he said, speaking slowly and shaking his head, "when I went to jail I had some money in my pocket—five dollars. When they searched me, they found it and tuck it away. I thought they were just agoin' to keep it for me." Then, shaking his head sadly, "But when I got out and got ready to come home today, I went to 'em for my money, and they said I couldn't have it, that I had to pay that on my board bill while I was in jail. Now there ain't so such law as that in North Carolina that they can put me in jail and then make me pay for my eatin', is there?"

"I don't know, Uncle Abe, whether there is or not," I said. "But I'll phone that clerk of the court and find out what he says." I thought I owed it to him, since I landed him in jail in the first place.

So I phoned. And the clerk of the court said that the jailer was exactly right—that Uncle Abe had to pay that five dollars on his board—and to tell Uncle Abe it was all according to law.

So I told Uncle Abe exactly what the jailer had said. He gave a little chuckle and said, "Well, I'd better give up arguin' 'bout it, I guess." And he started off. As he went up the hill from my house I stood in the door watching him. He turned around to me and he said, "Now you've done had your way. Don't you make no more fuss about this."

I said, "Uncle Abe, if you don't send that boy to school, history will certainly repeat itself. Now you know what that means?"

"I guess I do," he said, and he walked on.

History did not repeat itself, for the boy was a regular attendant at school after that.


# 18

BUT that wasn't the last time I saw Uncle Abe. Not by a jugful. It was to be many months later when once more Uncle Abe took a hand in school affairs.

But I'm getting ahead of the story.

After Hepsy went off to school at Banner Elk and a little later four others had followed her, we began seriously to get into the business of sending children off to high school, for we had no adequate high-school course at Crossnore, and more and more boys and girls were wanting to go on with their education.

When that session at Banner Elk was over, those girls came home and were so enthusiastic about school that in the fall sixteen begged to go. I promised I'd see to it that somehow they got a chance to do it. Then it began to be told about the country that if a child wanted to go to a more advanced school than we had at Crossnore or elsewhere in that part of the country, they could just come to me and make arrangements.

Old-clothes money had to do the work. Contributions grew and grew, so that Uncle Gilmer had to drive his old mule Rhoda from the post office to his home, hitched to the little one-horse wagon, in order to haul the big boxes and packages sent by friends from various sections down in the lower country. The people came from miles around to buy, so that we began to obtain sizable funds from the sales. And we kept sending children off to school.

But we realized, in one sense, that it was the wrong thing to do. It would be far better to keep those children at home and provide them a high school at Crossnore. That would benefit the entire community. So we determined to have our own high school, and we set our caps to get it. I might add that before we were able to establish a high school at Crossnore, the old-clothes money had sent off that last year one hundred and four boys and girls to other schools. From one girl—Hepsy—to one hundred and four youngsters, and in just a few years, is not a bad record, even if I do mention it myself.

But, as I said, we were anxious to get plans under way for having our own high school. As the sale of old clothes grew and the interest of the children in going away for more advanced schooling increased, it seemed that you could see the community developing an enthusiasm for education. We began to hold meetings to discuss plans.

We had held meetings in the old schoolhouse to talk about plans for moving it and building the two-room structure, and we had held similar meetings in the two-room building to talk expansion again. We were great for holding meetings.

I recall one particularly.

In those early days public meetings, even church meetings, often were the occasion for considerable disorder and sometimes actual bloodshed. Young men—and sometimes men not so young—would get themselves drunk on moonshine liquor and come to these meetings, oftentimes to wait for the meeting to end so they could walk their girls home. They would usually stay on the outside and frequently would get into altercations that sometimes ended in shooting.

We had had disorder at one of our school meetings and I was afraid that if such goings-on were not challenged, and challenged promptly, they would cause the more fearful and timid people to stay away, and that would very quickly end our movement for expanded school facilities.

So I made a plan, and I carried it out. I sent to Newland and got a deputy sheriff to agree to come over to Crossnore. Then I got three pistols and put them in my big handbag, and we went to the meeting, Doctor and I.

The deputy sheriff was there. And, of course, faithful Uncle Alex. I greeted the deputy sheriff and opened my big bag, so that everybody could see the pistols.

"Mr. Sheriff," I said, "we have been having disorder at our meetings, and this is against the law. I want you to deputize Uncle Alex and Doctor Sloop to help you maintain order here tonight."

The deputy sheriff had the two to raise their hands, and he swore them in. When he had done so I reached into my bag and brought out two pistols. I handed one to Doctor and the other to Uncle Alex.

"Now, gentlemen," I said, "in the name of the Lord and the State of North Carolina, I want you to shoot the first man who dares to interrupt our meeting. I'll handle this other pistol myself." I said it in a loud voice, too.

We called the meeting to order. And, brothers, it kept in order. Nobody offered to raise his voice, much less his shotgun or rifle. Those men very likely knew that the law wouldn't have allowed any of us to shoot just because someone had begun to talk loud or curse, but they didn't know that I knew it. And they weren't willing to risk Uncle Alex or Doctor or even the deputy sheriff. At any rate, the meeting proceeded in an orderly manner, even though, as I recall it now, a very heated argument developed between two fathers over the proposition of whether Crossnore School should teach that the world was round or flat.

A new North Carolina law greatly aided our efforts to get a high school. It decreed that any community could have a high school if it had a certain number of pupils in the high-school grades, provided the taxpayers of that community would vote on themselves a tax of thirty cents on the hundred dollars' property valuation to supplement the fund the state itself would provide toward the operation of a high school.

We had meetings, and we talked high school. We cornered little knots of people and talked high school. Before long the leaders in the community agreed that we should hold an election on the issue of voting the supplemental tax. They thought it would pass. So we called the election. And we began in earnest now to campaign in support of the tax. We chose two reliable and loyal politicians to go and visit all the homes in the school district. They went in different directions, and they covered the ground thoroughly. They came back with reports that many of the citizens were in favor of a high school and were willing to be taxed to support it, but they also had discovered quite a number who opposed the project. Then we knew that we really had a fight on our hands. Some days we'd get news that a convert had been made; on others we'd hear that folks just didn't want to be taxed that much. It would be a close vote.

So the morning came for the voting. They had put the two boxes out in front of the home of an old man who lived at the foot of a high hill directly west of the house. They grinned when I objected to the voting place—because that, I said, would make the sun set earlier and the voting was to stop, of course, at sunset. Several of those who favored the tax, I knew, lived at a considerable distance and I was afraid they might be late getting to the polls. But they wouldn't change the place, and I didn't know how to make them.

I was getting ready to go down to the voting place early that morning, when Dr. Sloop came back into the kitchen and told me that a neighbor had stopped by to say that he had been down at the voting place and that he didn't think that it would be safe for me to go. He said there were a great many men there from Buck Hill, that they were violently opposed to being taxed, and that every man had his gun. He was afraid there would be shooting before the day was over.

And Doctor said, "He advises you not to go."

105

I looked up at him and said, "And you know what I will do with his advice. Is the car ready?" For by that time we had a Model-T Ford.

He said, "Yes. You're going to risk it, are you?"

"It's not any risk," I replied. "Mountain men wouldn't shoot at me. You all don't respect them like I do. They won't hurt me one bit in the world."

We started off down the road. And though a Model-T was rather small then, and Doctor and I were never small, we passed two old people going down to vote, and the question was, Shall we pick them up? Doctor said, "They'll vote against us."

I said, "I can't help it. I'm not going to let them walk down there." So the old man got in and took his wife in his lap and we went on down the road. We cast our vote for the special tax, and they cast their vote against it.

The election officials told us that the vote was still tied, that it had been tied for an hour. They couldn't get anybody to break it. When one person voted for it, there was always somebody who came up and voted against it.

And so the vote stayed tied for a long, long time. We argued with all the people standing around. Some of them had voted, some of them hadn't. But none of them seemed willing to vote for it. One man that I felt sure would be in favor of it said, "No, I don't mind the tax. I want my children to get an education, but there ain't no sense in children having to go to school nine months in the year. Four months is long aplenty for them to be kept indoors."

So we grew more and more anxious. Finally Doctor said, "I'm going up to Lee's. I don't believe Lee will refuse to do me the favor of coming down here and voting in favor of it, and we'll break the tie."

He got into his little car and drove off. Pretty soon somebody said, "Where's Doctor?" I told them where.

"It won't do a bit o' good," they said. "Lee left the county

106

this morning before six o'clock. Said he couldn't never face Doctor and vote against it, and so he won't agoin' to be in the county this day."

Well, that made things look pretty serious. Then one man came up—and it was a man who had a little Ford too, a Model-T. It was in bad shape. I had always told him that he drove that Ford on will power—that it ran on will power, not on gasoline.

But he said to me, "Mrs. Sloop, I stopped at Uncle Abe's house last night and his sons were in there and they were all-fired mad about this tax being voted and were athreatenin' what they were agoin' to do if it was. Old Uncle Abe was alyin' in bed sick. But he said, 'If I could get up out o' this bed and get over there, I'd vote for it. I'd vote for anything that just woman said.'

"Now if I could go over there," he added, "I believe I could get Uncle Abe to come vote."

"Do you think he'd be able to come?" I asked him.

"Oh, yes," he said, "it wouldn't hurt him none. But he can't walk it, and they wouldn't bring him any other way."

He started to get in his car, turned around to me again. "I feel sure he'll come. You just pray that he will be awillin' to risk it."

I said, "I'll pray that your tires will last over that road, for there's never been an automobile over it."

"That's what they tell me," he said, "but we'll be acomin' back."

And he got in, and with its usual will power that little car started off, and I certainly prayed for those tires.

In just a little while before the sun was to set behind that high hill, he came back. The tires had held, the little car was still chugging, and Uncle Abe stepped out.

"Where's your box?" he said.

I didn't dare speak to him, because they'd say I had influenced him to vote. And I stepped back.

The registrar who was holding the election showed him where the box was. So he went over there, and they fixed his vote for him, and he put it in the box marked FOR. Then he turned slowly and walked back to the car. I stepped up to thank him.

"Uncle Abe," I said, "we appreciate your aid ever so much."

He looked right straight at me and said, "Hunn-n-h-h!" And he got in the car.

I never saw Uncle Abe again.

In a few moments a bearded man came up. I held my breath. Was he going to tie the vote again? "Waal-l-l," he said, "I ain't voted yet, but since Abe has give 'em the vote, I guess I'll add another one to it and make it two in majority."

We had voted our high school.

## 19

WE had voted the supplementary school tax, I had the land and lumber for which I had been offered four thousand dollars, and I knew that Avery County would provide some of the necessary funds for building the proposed new school. But I knew too that we were still a long way from seeing the completed structure standing up there on the hillside.

The plans had been sketched out and they had estimated the building would cost twenty-six thousand dollars. That much money in those days in Avery County was a fabulous sum. People just didn't figure there was that much money in the world. And to put all that into a school building!

The mountain people had such a pitifully small income. And a large part of the little money they received came from liquor making. I was dead set against liquor, and they knew it. Our relentless hostility to moonshining and everything related to liquor making and liquor drinking we had brought with us to Crossnore when we came over from Plum-tree. We had fought it there, and we continued to fight it here. Everybody understood our stand on liquor. We talked against it and prayed against it and did everything we knew to fight it. I kept after the sheriff and the deputies so much that they hated to see me coming, I know.

Liquor was bad for everybody, but it was particularly bad for the young people, and I was especially interested in these young folks. I railed against the older men's teaching the youngsters to drink moonshine liquor and to make it. I told them it was an outrageous thing to do. Many young boys would help their daddies or uncles at the stills at night. Now and then they'd get in fights, and sometimes there were killings. We didn't have feud murders in our area, but we had liquor murders. Yes, that's what they were. These boys and sometimes the old men would get drunk and start arguing and quarreling, and the first thing you knew there'd be shooting.

Lots of times, too, when the men got to drinking, they'd fall out about the land boundaries. Sometimes they weren't even drinking when they fell out because of land. In the mountains people took great pride in owning land and if a man "got over" on his neighbor's land there might be a fight and a killing as a result. "That land b'longed to my daddy and my granddaddy afore him and my daddy's granddaddy afore them," a man would say; "and I don't aim to let nobody take it away from me." Sometimes, too, if the man wasn't especially courageous, he might take a drink of moonshine liquor before he went calling on the neighbor to settle their difficulty. "If'n I can get a quart under my shirt," he'd say, "I'll stand right up to him. He ain't agoin' to have none o' my land."

And if he'd had enough moonshine to bolster up his courage, there might be shooting. And now and then somebody got killed—usually because of liquor. Occasionally it might be a boy in his teens who was killed, a boy who should have been in school and not out at a still.

In making our fight for better school facilities and better teaching I pointed out that education and liquor just didn't go along together. And as we worked for the building of the little two-room school and the subsequent additions to it, as we struggled to build Treasure Island and the Wart, as we campaigned for the passage of the tax proposal for the support of our projected high school, I fought liquor with every means I could devise. And we had many exciting experiences.

One Sunday morning—and I shall never forget it—a message came to me. It was during World War I, I recall, perhaps late in 1917 or maybe early the next year. It was a very secret message. I mustn't tell anybody. But this man had found out where there was a still. He said they had moved it, but he believed it could be found right close around. He said the place was "part the way up Still Branch." He thought maybe I'd want to send somebody up there and get that still.

The reason they called that little stream Still Branch was because it was such a fine stream for liquor making, and there's no telling how many stills have been located on it. It ran along through rocks that at many places provided excellent locations for stills. They said you could get a third more liquor from your mash on Still Branch than on other streams, and that was because the water was so cold that it made for faster condensation and speeded the distilling process. . . . Oh, yes, I know all about it. When you fight something, you have to know.

Now it happened that Doctor had bought that piece of land that had Still Branch on it. So the moonshiners had been afraid to set up on it. But these men, the men told me, felt that we wouldn't suspect them since it had been so long since there had been a still on Still Branch. So they had put one on it.

They had made a web around it of fine black thread which didn't show in the grass. In that way they could come back, after having been away for hours, and tell if anybody had been near their still. The web would be broken if anybody had come prowling around.

Sure enough, they had found the web broken. So they had moved the still. But they hadn't carried it far away. They had taken it across a little bridge and hid it behind a big log and piled some brush on it. Then they had slipped away. This we learned later, of course.

Doctor Sloop was not at home that day, but he had said he'd be back by nightfall. It had begun to rain.

I sent for Uncle Alex and another man in the community and told them of the situation and asked them if they were willing to go with Doctor to hunt that still that night. "Yes," they said, "we will."

"But I ain't got no pistol," one of them said.

I said, "Well, you're welcome to use mine."

"All right," he answered. "I will."

So I brought out our three pistols, and we cleaned them —they were pretty clean anyhow—and I found the ammunition for them. Then I got the lantern and fixed it with a dark side. They said they would return to our house about dark, and left. When Doctor came in I told him what was waiting for him. So I fed him just as quickly as possible, and soon the two men returned, and the three started off—with my blessings and my earnest prayers that nothing would happen to them.

They searched that place everywhere. They could see where the still had been. There was a little mash left there, and some meal, and a quantity of molasses that was being used instead of sugar. They turned all that out—destroyed everything. But they could not find the still. So they came home.

"We found where the still had been," Doctor reported,

111

"but we couldn't find it." They had got close, but just hadn't gone far enough, they learned later.

"Well," I said, "we'll try something else tomorrow."

The next day I asked one man if he'd go, and he said, "No." He was afraid. He said, "They ain't atalkin' 'bout nothin' else around here now but that still."

"But," I said, "we must get that thing. They'll bring it out again just as soon as we quiet down, and we mustn't quiet down till we find it."

But he wouldn't go.

I went to the telephone and called up another and asked him if he didn't want to go on an errand for me that night.

He said, "I think I know what you're atalkin' 'bout. Everybody else's atalkin' 'bout it." He didn't want to go.

I said, "Well, all right. We'll do something about it; I don't know what, but we'll do something."

Just then Walt came in. Walt was a deputy sheriff. I knew that he had been accused of dealing in liquor, and I knew he drank it.

"What can I do for you?" I asked him.

He said, "I've got somethin' to tell you, and I expect it will surprise you. I know who those men were who went for that still last night." He didn't tell me that he was over there watching. But that's what he had been doing, I was sure. "I know exactly where that still is," he said. "What'll you give me for gettin' it? And who'll you send out there with me?"

"There's not a man in this country that hasn't got feathers on his legs," I said, "except Doctor. But *I'll* go with you to get that still, and I'm no man."

He said, "You know you wouldn't."

I said, "I'll show you."

I went in the house and got a red sweater and put it on. I wore it a lot, and I thought they'd recognize me. I told him I'd get the wheelbarrow.

"We can't tote it," he said; "it's a big still—a 125-gallon one."

"I don't know anything about the size of 'em."

"It's good copper, too," he said. Walt seemed to know a lot about it.

"All right," I told him, "I'll get the wheelbarrow and I'll go."

"You better let me go ahead," he said, "and get it down to the place where the wheelbarrow can go. We can roll it down the hill from there. But first there's a lot of stumps I'll have to heave it over. I'll get it down to the wheelbarrow by the time you get there. You ain't ascared to go, you sure?"

"No, I'm not afraid," I told him.

"You ain't ascared to go by yourself?"

"Of course I'm not. I'm not going by myself anyway; I'm on the Lord's business."

But I still couldn't understand what Walt was doing being interested in getting the still for me. Later somebody said to me, "Weren't you ascared he was agoin' to get you over there and capture you in some way or another?"

"No," I said. "It never occurred to me that anybody would want me."

He went on ahead, and I started up toward the gap to turn out on the road that went to the dam—over where the Still Branch was—and I met a teacher, a pretty young thing from Kentucky, and she said, "Where are you going? I wanted to come see you."

"I'm on an important errand," I said.

She said, "Where are you going?"

I said, "I'm going to get a still."

"Oh, let me go with you," she said. I could see she was excited.

I said, "Yes, I knew you were the right one. You came from Kentucky; you know a lot about stills. But you'll spoil that pretty skirt you've got on."

113

"I'll sacrifice it to help capture a still," she declared.

So we went on together toward Still Branch. She rolled the wheelbarrow part of the way, and I rolled it part of the way. It was just a narrow walking trail, not wide enough for two to walk abreast, just wide enough for one, and it ran along the side of a hill. We kept the wheelbarrow going; at one or two places it was about to tumble over, but she'd get under it and hold it so it wouldn't tip, and I'd push. So we went on until we got to the place where Walt had told me to stop, and sure enough, there he was, heaving the still over the last obstacle.

So we loaded it onto the wheelbarrow. He said, "Now you hold it steady and I'll roll it."

"No, sir," I said. "If I roll it I'll walk in the path, but whoever holds it has got to walk on that steep hillside, and that's not going to be me."

So he got on one side, and she got on the other, and with me pushing the wheelbarrow we came around that hill with the still, and after a while we came out on the road.

Walt didn't know it, of course, but right after he left me to go to get the still I called Doctor, who was over in Newland examining boys for the Army. I said to him, "I've found the thing you couldn't find last night. At least, I've found a man who knows where it is, and we're going after it."

"What are you going to do with it?" he asked me.

"I'm going to bring it out here and put it in the back of your car, and you're going to drive it into Newland and put it in the vault at the bank until tomorrow. There's lots of talk about it. But I want that still to go to court."

"But I can't get there," Doctor said. "These boys have got to go home and by the time I get through examining them it'll be late at night before they get home."

"Let 'em hunt possums on the way," I said facetiously; "but, boys or no boys, you're going to take this still into Newland tonight."

He said, "I think you'd better try to hide it around home until tomorrow, and then I'll take it in."

"Well, all right," I said, "if you don't want to come for it, you needn't; but you can look out your window in about an hour, and you'll see me rolling that wheelbarrow into Newland with the still on it."

He said, "You wouldn't."

I said, "I will," And I hung up.

Newland is six miles away. I had walked to Newland before. That was no walk for me. Law, Miss Caroline Horton, one of our registered nurses, walked to Newland on her eightieth birthday to have her hair fixed. Yes, she did. Somebody brought her back, but she walked over there. I would have rolled that still over there too. Yes, I would.

But when we came around the edge of the hill and got in sight of the road, there was Doctor in his car.

I said, "This is grand."

"What are you going to do with it?" he asked me.

"I'm going to put it in the back of your car," I said. We had a rumble seat in the back of the car.

"You are going to cover it up, aren't you?" he asked.

I said, "You can if you want to."

"Well," he said, "I'll put my slicker around it."

"All right," I agreed. "That'll be all right; you put your slicker over it."

So we put the still in the rumble seat of the car and tied it so it wouldn't fall off. "I think I'd better go in the house a minute," Doctor said, when everything was ready.

He went into the house and came back with his pistol—a .45. He laid it down on the seat beside him. "Walter," he said to the deputy sheriff, "you want to go to Newland with me?"

"Yes, sir," he said, "I'll be glad to."

Walt was certainly being agreeable. Then I saw the light. That was Walt's still! He had helped us capture his own

115

still. Or if not his alone, certainly it was his in partnership with somebody else. He had known that Doctor and the others had been on a hunt for the still, and he had felt sure we'd eventually find it, maybe catch him red-handed at it. And he a deputy sheriff!

So he had told me the story that he had come on it, thinking that he'd throw us off his trail. But if not that, then he'd be so cooperative and agreeable that he'd put us so much in his debt that we wouldn't have the heart to prosecute him.

But I didn't say anything, and Doctor and Walt got in the car and drove toward Newland.

They hadn't been gone more than five minutes when I heard three loud pistol shots, one right after another. In the mountains that means a still has been captured, and if you have anything to do with it, make tracks out of the country. I learned later who fired those three shots. The man had seen Doctor go by and recognized him, and he knew by the shape of the thing under the slicker that it was a still; he knew too that I had been on the hunt of a still, and he knew that Doctor had been one of those who had been looking for it the night before. There weren't but two or three cars in our part of the country in those days and Doctor had one of them; so he recognized Doctor and saw through the whole thing, and he was up for telling his friends, and that's what the pistol shots had meant. But the funny thing was that he didn't know that the owner—or one of the owners—of the still was sitting up there in the car beside Doctor.

They took the still to the bank—the courthouse by that time was closed—and the next day the sheriff came and got it and took it right out on the street at Newland and broke it up as the law provided and in accordance with the custom.

And I never went anywhere for so long a time but what somebody would tell me something about *my* still.

# 20

NOT long after we "captured" that still—it must have been before World War I had ended—we got a certain man here at Crossnore to be a deputy sheriff. I knew he would be a good one, and we persuaded him to take the place. The sheriff said he would appoint him, and he did.

There was another still that we were looking for. We knew that the man who had that still was making liquor all the time, and we were determined to discover it, but we just hadn't been able to do so. I talked to a lot of the women that went galacking—they were picking galax leaves, which sold well to people in the lower country for decorations—and some of them would tell me what they knew if I'd declare I wouldn't tell where I got my information. They had tried me out, and they knew I wouldn't.

But this still I just couldn't find.

Then one day this new deputy told me that he thought he had some straight information. "I believe," he said, "that I've got a line on where that still is, and I'm going after it tomorrow."

"All right," I said. "Good luck to you."

The next day was commencement day at Crossnore, and I was sitting up on the rostrum for the commencement exercises. We were seated in a semicircle and I was at the end, next to the edge of the platform. I was to introduce the speaker, who was a big education man from down in Raleigh.

Then I saw this deputy come in. He looked sort of disheveled. I just knew where he'd been. He walked right straight up to me. "I need you to come outside a minute," he said, "and I think we'd better go to your house."

I asked, "Why? Did you get it?"

"Yes," he said.

I said, "All right. Is it outside?"

He nodded.

"I'll have to be excused for a few minutes," I told the principal. I went outside, and there it was. It was another big one.

"It's too late to carry it off today," he said, "and I got no place to put it. But if you'll take it home and hide it, then I'll take it out early tomorrow morning, and we'll get it over to Newland."

"Yes," I said, "I'll take it home; I'm not afraid of keeping it. But I don't know where I'll hide it. My house is not a very good hiding place. But we'll go try."

So I climbed in the wagon with him and the still. It was in the back, and there was some straw over it; it surely was a big one, too. We went to my house.

I had a pretty good-sized closet, but all my clothes and my family's clothes were hanging in that closet. We looked in it. He said, "That's fine. The clothes will cover up the still."

So we took the still out and put it in there. We even got the cap, and we put it in the closet too. Lots of times in raiding a still you couldn't find the cap, for they would bury the cap before they would let you have that. We closed the closet, and I locked the house up tight as I could. Then I went on down to the commencement and introduced the education man from Raleigh.

The next day I put on a dress that came out of that closet, and about that time somebody knocked on the door. I went to the door, and there was one of the neighbors. She sniffed. "You haven't started to drinking liquor, have you?" she asked.

"Why, no," I said, a bit indignantly, "I don't drink. You know that!"

"Well, you sure do smell like liquor," she said.

And for the longest time Doctor and I—and the children—all smelled like liquor everywhere we went. I just couldn't get the smell out of those clothes. I hung them up all over

118

the place, but the liquor smell stayed in them for a long time.

The day after we put the still in the closet they took it to Newland and broke it up, while the crowd watched, some of them sadly, I'm sure. And once more the news got around, and folks would come to me and say, "Well, Mis' Sloop, I hears they busted up another one of your stills."

The capture of this second still happened just after Doctor had got his little electric-light plant started. It was just a little dam then, and there wasn't enough water in dry weather. So Doctor would turn it off during the day and let the water catch up, and then he'd turn it on again when it came toward night. On this particular occasion he had turned it off.

Doctor had taught one of the men who worked with him how to go out to the dam and turn the power on. So I got word to the man that he'd have to turn on the lights that evening, as Doctor would be away. He came up to the house.

"Mrs. Sloop," he said, "I don't mind aturnin' on them lights as a usual thing. But I'm ascared to go up to that place tonight. You know since you all captured that still, I'm ascared to go up there."

"Yes, we got the still," I said, "but what's that got to do with turning on the lights?"

He said, "Don't you know that when you go around that trail on the side of that mountain ferninst them woods over acrost the hollow there—don't you know that's just the place for somebody to hide and shoot at you? And they'll think I'm Doctor going out to turn on the lights, don't you know? It's agittin' on toward evenin', and I'm just ascared to go."

"Aw, bosh!" I said. "I've never heard of such a thing. Give me my red sweater, and I'll walk in front of you and he won't see you; he'll see me. There won't be a pistol ball go through me, and I know it!"

And I did. I walked every foot of the mile out there with him, and he was behind me so he wouldn't show and they'd shoot at me. And, just as I said, there was not a pistol shot fired.


## 21

WE realized from the time we came up into this country that it needed many things. We saw that it was indeed poor in many aspects, though we saw too that it was rich in others. This little county of Avery, named for old General Avery who lost his life in a skirmish in the Revolutionary War on a spot of land now within the confines of the county, had a pitifully small total taxable valuation, and how could it build new schools? How could they put up comfortable, cheerful homes?—the strength and security of any community.

It was easy to see that what this country must have before it could really prosper was the development of a better way of earning an income. Farm crops were the district's main product. But with no roads, Avery County would remain isolated; with no prospect of moving their crops and selling them to the outside world, the farmers would continue to fail in achieving prosperity.

Nor would they even achieve good health. Their diet, we soon discovered, as a general thing was atrocious. The routine meals of many of our families lacked even the rudiments of proper balance. Few homes ever had any food that hadn't been raised on the place. But worse, often they didn't eat what they raised, many of them, and what they ate was very poorly cooked.

We discovered that they were eating much hog meat, winter and summer. One day during hog-killing time I saw at one small mountain-cabin home nine hogs swung up after they had been slaughtered. And little if any of that meat was sold. The family ate those nine hogs! Often the men and boys would kill deer and bears, but they preferred to sell this meat and eat the hog meat.

Each family usually raised some vegetables, such as corn, cabbage, onions, Irish potatoes, and sorghum (made from molasses cane), but frequently the men of the family ate only bread and meat, and the vegetables, when used at all, were badly cooked. Mountain women usually had these vegetables simply floating in hog lard, and the things that they fried were sopping with grease. One old gentleman told me once that not one day that year past had he missed having his buckwheat cakes for breakfast. He had cooked them himself, and he had fried them in hog lard and drowned them in thick sweet sorghum.

There was one man up in our country, though, who didn't eat all his hog meat. Each year he had gone down to Salisbury in the late fall or early winter and taken two or three hams to a man who ran a haberdashery store there. This storekeeper had been his regular customer for ten or twelve years or maybe longer. So one day, when our citizen arrived with the hams the storekeeper greeted him cordially, told him how good the last year's hams had been and how much he appreciated the mountain man's faithfulness in supplying him each year.

"I know I have been paying you for the hams, but I want to do something extra to show my appreciation for the way you have looked after me all these years," he said. "The other day I got in a new batch of nice felt hats. I want to give you a new hat and also one for each one of your boys."

The man from Crossnore was delighted, and he thanked the merchant profusely.

"Well," the merchant went on, "you've been good to me. I figure that's mighty little to do for you in return. Now tell me what size hat you wear and also what sizes your boys wear. I want each one of your boys to have a nice hat that fits him." He smiled. "By the way, how many boys you got?"

"I got twenty-five boys," the Crossnore man replied. "With me, that'll be twenty-six hats."

The merchant stood silent a moment, aghast. "But I don't have but twenty-six hats in the store," he finally managed to say.

"Waal," the mountain man drawled, "I'd hate to take all you got. You jus' fix up them boys and I won't take none for myself. I'll jus' keep on a-wearin' my old coonskin cap."

But speaking about what the mountain people used to eat back in those early days reminds me of Uncle War Clark. His name was Warsaw—his mother named him from the book *Thaddeus of Warsaw*—but everybody called him Uncle War. Uncle War was a brother of Uncle Newt and a son of Uncle Drew. Uncle Drew Clark was one of nine sons, seven of whom had names starting with the letter *d:* Drewery (Uncle Drew), Dothan, Douthard (called Douth), Detroy, Dalas, De Eston, Dolphus. I was talking one day with Uncle War, and I told him that I supposed that if his mother had had another son she'd have been bound to name him Damn.

Uncle War once said to me, "Mis' Sloops, that thing you l'arn them young 'uns up at the schoolhouse ain't music. If you want to hear real music, you listen to the music of them hounds abayin' as they hunt on the hillsides. That's music!" And I agreed.

But I started off to tell more about the diet of the mountain people when we came into this country. Uncle War was telling me about customs at his father's house.

"My father had fourteen sons, and he adopted fourteen more boys," he told me. "He al'ays wanted a lot of boys around."

"Did he have any daughters, Uncle War?" I asked.

"Yes," he said, "there was Nora and Cora and Cordelia. Their names all ended with the same letter, you see, the letter *a.*"

"Well," I said, "the girls must have had a hard life."

"Well," he said, "I don't see why. How do you figure that?"

"Cooking for all those men and boys," I said. "How'd they ever do it?"

"Oh," he said, "that never bothered them much. All they had to do was to keep enough bread cooked and on the shelf. We never set down to eat like folks do now, but when we felt the urge to eat we just went by the shelf and got us a hunk of bread and went on out to the smokehouse and cut us a piece o' meat and whittled and et as we walked."

"You mean the meat wasn't cooked?" I asked.

"It was smoked when we put it up in the smokehouse," he replied, with a trace of impatience. "When fall come every year, Pa he'd say, 'Boys, git yo' guns and start out, and fill her full!' He was talkin' about afillin' the smokehouse with meat. And that's what we done."

"What kind of meat, Uncle War?"

"Bears, and deers, and wild hawgs, and possums and coons and rabbits, all kinds of game meat," he said. "We'd leave one of the boys at the smokehouse to keep the fire agoin' and we'd fill that smokehouse plumb to the rafters. And then we'd have meat to eat all winter and the next summer and till we started ahuntin' again."

"But didn't you eat any vegetables, Uncle War?" I asked.

"Well, the wimmenfolks sometimes raised a little garden sass, but they never could git us to eat none. We'd eat a onion now and then and turnips if'n they was raw. But we never et none cooked. We was al'ays satisfied to eat dried meat with that bread from the shelf."

I could vouch for the way they ate onions and turnips. Uncle War might have added that they didn't even bother to wash them. I've seen many a man pull up a turnip, whisk it under his arm a time or two to clean off the dirt, and then start eating, sometimes without bothering to peel it.

By modern standards their diets and eating habits were terrible. The thing I can't understand—if good food has anything to do with long life—is how they grew to be so old. Uncle War, for instance. He had four wives, I have been told. The first wife presented him two daughters, Pet and Dumps, the second had no children, the third, a widow, had six or eight when he married her, and the fourth, whom he married at the age of ninety-one, made him the very proud father of two. I remember that when Uncle War was ninety-eight, we had some sort of a church meeting one night, and he, as the oldest man there, was presented a Bible.

I can't recommend the diet under which Uncle War grew up, but if one looks at results, it's hard to say much against that bread-and-smoked-meat routine.

As we learned more about the living habits of the people of the mountains and realized that they had little prospects of improving their situations unless something could be done to make our mountain region less isolated, we began to give much thought to the problem.

The thing to do, we decided, was to learn first what could be raised to advantage and then to fight for good roads that would enable our people to take their crops to market. I well remember the shock—yes, it was actually a shock—I had one day and how sharply it pointed up the situation when a man in our community said to me, "I made a mistake. I planted too many potatoes; I'm going to have nigh on to forty bushel left over."

"Why, Mr. Jim," I said, "that's an advantage. You can sell those potatoes."

"Sell Irish potatoes!" he said incredulously. "Who ever heard of anybody who'd buy an Irish potato?"

"Well," I said, "they do buy a lot of 'em down in my country."

"But I can't git to it. I'd tear my wagon to pieces to go over them roads."

So they couldn't sell what they grew, and some of it was

awfully good, though some was poor for lack of knowledge of how to handle the land and how to handle their fertilizers. So I wrote down to the State Department of Agriculture and asked them to send us a man up here who would talk to our people about the suitable crops for this climate. We're 3400 feet above sea level, and it's bitterly cold here in the winter; it dips to zero, and I've seen it go to fifteen below. We didn't have any way of taking care of the chickens, of preventing their freezing. I used to say that every chicken I bought after Christmas had no toes and no comb. We were handicapped in every way. The cows were not milked during the winter but were turned loose to rustle for themselves. The people, the little children, went without milk when they needed it most.

We must have something better, a better prospect, I told myself, and I talked it among the people. We must have better homes than the little boarded-up cabins huddling along the hillsides or down in the coves. So many of them had cracks in the walls through which the wind would whistle; and that's why families were so eager to get hold of magazines, so they could pull out the leaves and paste them on the walls. We must do better, I told them. We must find a way, and we must *want to* do better.

Pretty soon, in answer to my letter two men came from Raleigh. One of them was a most enthusiastic poultryman. But he shook his head and said, "This country won't do for poultry raising."

And we knew it wouldn't.

The other man asked, "What is your best crop here?"

I said, "The best-tasting crop is the Irish-potato crop. They're the best-tasting Irish potatoes I've ever seen."

"Well, now," he said, "that might not be bad. What's the elevation of this valley?"

I referred him to Dr. Sloop, and Doctor said, "The lowest point is at Linville Falls, and that's 3200 feet above sea level."

"Why, man," he said, "you've got a gold mine here!"

We all perked up our ears.

"You know," he went on, "all the potato dealers buy their seed potatoes from Maine. They speak of planting Maine potatoes. That's because Maine is the only state east of the Rockies that has farms that are 3000 feet above sea level, and good seed potatoes must be raised 3000 feet above sea level. Here you have a whole valley that's 3200 feet and more above sea level. Why, you ought to grow the best seed potatoes in the world!"

How we did begin to listen to that man from the Department of Agriculture! He was speaking at a mass meeting, and everybody in our section of the mountains had turned out— men and women and children and babies! Potatoes were something we knew about. There was hope.

And so our region became interested in potatoes as a revenue crop. Before long two or three of the men who very carefully had followed direct instructions had raised a plot of potatoes from which they sent some to Washington to be tested. Then Washington planted them in their test gardens. Our potatoes turned out better than the Maine potatoes!

That was our chance. We began to learn potato raising all over the country, and we began to raise potatoes. But, oh, we couldn't do anything with them. They had to be holed in in great pits dug in the earth and the dirt piled on them to keep them from freezing in the winter, and we could take them out in fairly good condition in late March or early April when the farmers down the country wanted to begin to plant. But by the time we put them in the wagon and dragged them a whole day over those rough roads they were chilled, and often they disappointed the farmers who bought them in the hope that they were getting first-rate seed potatoes.

We just had to have better roads.

And so we began sending delegations out to road meetings, and finally I was invited to come to Raleigh for a meeting of the legislature—to stay six weeks and work with the Good Roads Committee of North Carolina to put through a bill which would give us fifty million dollars with which to build schools and roads, real roads. That was at the beginning of the 1920s, during the administration of Governor Cameron Morrison of Charlotte, who was so heartily in favor of good roads and good schools.

How we did work!—getting out letters, writing questions to other states, doing everything we could to make that bill acceptable to the legislators. I talked to mountain representatives day in and day out to show them that it was a worthwhile bill and would mean more to them than to any other people in the whole state. And to a man they voted for it!

One mountain man even wanted to make it a hundred million dollars. But they nearly mobbed him when he suggested that!

Gradually we built the roads. It took work, it took vigilance, it took constant pushing to get them. Every other community wanted roads, and Crossnore was so little and so isolated, and the roads to Crossnore would be so expensive to build. But the roads had to be built!

And so, year in and year out, I—and oftentimes the Doctor—would hear of a road meeting that was going to be held that might influence the building of our roads in Avery County. Sometimes we would go together; other times I would mount my horse and go to the nearest railroad station, leave the horse there, and go on to the road meeting. And there I'd fight to show them that Crossnore was going to have a future, that Crossnore was going to have people enough in the country around it to be worthy of a road, that Avery County needed a road on the eastern side of the Blue Ridge that would go from north to south of the county.

One road commissioner said in a meeting, "It seems like Mrs. Sloop thinks that Avery County rates twins. They've got a good road from one end of the county to the other—from

Elk Park on down to the southern edge of the county. Why should they want another road to parallel it on the eastern side of the county?"

My answer to him was that I had always felt that the Lord controlled the coming of twins, and so He had made twin roads necessary in Avery County by putting the Blue Ridge through the county from north to south with very little connection between the two sides, and that we on the eastern side were not helped materially by the road on the western side of the Blue Ridge. I insisted that we ought to have that road.

Finally the day came when they agreed to give it to us. I'll never forget that time. Many a day I had passed out from the foot of the mountain where there was an old blacksmith shop and an old man always sitting in front of it. I never saw him at work. He would always stop me and talk, and I'd always tell him I was going after that good road. One day, shortly before we were granted the road, I had said to him, "I'm going after that good road, and I'm going to bring it back in my saddle pockets."

He turned around to a fellow who was there. "You know," he said, "I've always said that I'd die before I'd vote the Democratic ticket, but when she runs for President I aim to vote for her."

That was the highest compliment I ever had paid to me!

Then in a few days the road-building machine did come. It scared the old man to death, and he went in his shop and shut himself up because he knew it was the Devil! But the driver of the machine was a very patient man. He got down and went in to see the old blacksmith. He told him that if he'd come out and look at it, he'd surely be interested. Otherwise the blacksmith would just have to remain miserable, for that machine was to work a long time right in front of his shop.

128

He was soon converted, like many another who was opposed to having a road put through his land, and finally we had a good road all the way up the mountain. They called it "Mis' Sloop's Road."

That road so helped to open up the country that we are now all raising beans, Irish potatoes, and cabbages for sale. The trucks can come to us for the produce our farmers raise, probably with the exception of the cabbages, which the farmers themselves generally haul to market. These are picked in the morning—cut, they call it, from their stems—packed in bags until the truck is mounded high. They start out in the late afternoon and without ever the sun reaching them are delivered in some part of the state or nearby states by sunup the next morning. They are really crisp mountain cabbages and can be sold for that.

We also are finding excellent markets now for our potatoes. They have become widely known as unusually fine potatoes —just as good as any in the world, in fact. It is in the Southeastern United States that the Avery County potatoes are sold, to a large extent. The government has solved our problem and furnished us with two large potato warehouses in which the potatoes can be kept safely through the winter after they've been carefully graded, and then they are sold to truckers and taken down the country.

Potatoes are our main crop, though the beans do bring in a good amount of money. The bean crop is more variable than the potato. The beans come on up here after the beans in the low country have burnt up in the heat of the summer. Now we have the big bean sheds where the beans are sold to trucks just as the tobacco is sold in the lower sections.

On one occasion, I recall, a man reported to me what a good price he had got for his beans. He said he had seen trucks standing there from the states of Texas and New York and all in between—waiting for his Avery County beans.

## 22

IT is amazing, indeed, to contemplate the change in our economic condition in Linville Valley. And it may seem strange to this new generation of million-dollar super high schools to learn how difficult it was for us to build our high school at Crossnore more than three decades ago.

But it was a task, and one I shall never forget, though I look back upon those days with deep pleasure and a sense of nostalgia.

We had so little to go on then.

But we had determined, earnest people who didn't know what the word quit meant. So we agreed we would build our big high school on the hillside, and we went to work.

As I said, it had been estimated that the structure would cost twenty-six thousand dollars. All we had, for certain, was four thousand dollars' worth of lumber and the promise of the Avery County school board to help us. We soon discovered that we wouldn't get much help from that source. But we kept after the board members, and finally they agreed to give us three thousand dollars. That was a huge sum, they all agreed. In fact, it was an almost unbelievable sum to give one school. I doubt if they'd ever given more than a thousand dollars to a school—at one clip.

So we started off with that lumber and three thousand dollars to build a schoolhouse big enough for both the elementary school and the high school. Of course, in those days seven thousand dollars was a lot of money.

But we were also given a great deal of cooperation by the neighbors, and many, many hours of free labor. I calculated once that the wages, if they had been paid—and some of the men worked for fifty cents a day, and some for even less—of all those people who swarmed there to help us cut down the side of that hill and make it level for the schoolhouse would have amounted to some five hundred dollars. That doesn't sound large today, of course, but then it would have paid the wages of three men working for more than a year! That was the day when a man and his horse—with the man providing his horse's feed, and his own, too—got a dollar and a quarter for a hard day's work.

In preparing the site for the schoolhouse, we had to do all the work with pick and shovel and those horse-drawn shovels—drag pans, they called them. That was long before they began using bulldozers and other big earth-moving contraptions.

But not all the work was given free of charge by the men—they couldn't afford to do that—and on Saturday afternoons I would go down to the site and write the checks for the work done that week. One Saturday afternoon we had been hauling cement from nearby Pineola, and the checks were rather bigger than usual. All the men came up to get theirs except Uncle Newt Clark. He stood back.

"Uncle Newt," I said, "you haven't got your check. Come up and I'll write it for you."

"No, you ain't agoin' to pay me no check," Uncle Newt said.

"But," I told him, "you've been working all week, and you're due your pay."

"I ain't agoin' to take no pay," he said firmly. "You come here to give our young 'uns a better school, and me and Mary Jane"—she was his wife—"said from the very start that you weren't agoin' to pay us for anything we do. But I'd like to aks you a question if you don't mind."

I said, "All right, Uncle Newt. What's that?"

He said, looking up the hill toward the rising schoolhouse, "What does you mean by a 'high school'? 'Pears to me like all our schools is high." And his eyes twinkled.

I said, "Yes, Uncle Newt, they are high. But a high school

means more advanced subjects. The children don't study the same things in high school that they do in the lower grades. They go further. They are nearer college education then."

The light shot into his eyes with a flash, and he said with bated breath: "Mis' Sloops, does you mean you teaches Latin?"

Looking at Uncle Newt you wouldn't have supposed he was interested in Latin. And so I made bold to ask the question: "Uncle Newt, yes, we will teach Latin. But what do you know about Latin?"

He said, "'Cause our folks from the Old Country writes to us that we're settled here in this lonely place, and we've got to be sure to get our young 'uns educated, and that nobody is educated that don't know Latin. So we've always wanted 'em to have Latin, and I'm agoin' home and tell Mary Jane they're agoin' to have Latin."

He went off with great happiness and without his check.

We kept on working to build that schoolhouse. I scrimped and saved and doled out the money, but it just wouldn't last. The men and the boys and sometimes the women worked and often without pay, but it seemed that we just couldn't complete it. I went to see the county-school-board members, but I couldn't prevail upon them to give us another cent. They were not used to giving out large sums; the county was very poor, as I have explained, and there was precious little money to be had.

One day I counted what was left and it wasn't much. I went down to the schoolhouse and told the men that they'd just have to quit the next Saturday; the money would be gone. We'd start back when we could find some funds. It almost broke my heart, but there was nothing else to do.

That was early in the week. Next Thursday when I saw the mailman hang our oilcloth mail bag on the old horseshoe nailed to the tree near the gate, I went up and got the bag, emptied it, and found several letters. The first one I opened was from a Mr. McGillican of New Orleans. He was a wealthy man down there, and was a friend of Crossnore. He said he wanted to do something for us, and so he was sending us a check for five thousand dollars! But that wasn't all. He went on to say that while he was writing his check, one of his friends had come in and he had induced him to write us a check for one thousand dollars. And two other friends had added checks—one for five hundred dollars and the other for two hundred and fifty dollars!

I ran all the way to the schoolhouse.

"Keep working, men!" I shouted. "We don't have to stop Saturday! I've got some money, and we can keep going!"

So the work continued day after day, and we were making fine progress. But after a while that New Orleans money ran out, and it looked like we'd have to stop.

I went to our local school board and asked them to borrow ten thousand dollars and sign their names to the note.

They read my title clear. They said I was a crazy woman. Borrow ten thousand dollars! It was preposterous. I had lost what sense I had, if I'd ever had any!

"Well, if you all won't borrow it, I will!" I told them.

They laughed then. Just try to, they said, though not out loud. But that's what they were saying to themselves, I could tell.

So I went to Mr. Guy, president of the Avery County Bank at Newland.

"Mr. Guy," I said, "I'm trying to get the schoolhouse finished. We've run out of money. I want to borrow ten thousand dollars."

"On what security, Mrs. Sloop?" the bank president asked.

"On my face," I told him.

He laughed. "Mrs. Sloop," he said, "I'll let you have it—on your face."

There were some red faces when I took that money back

to Crossnore and started those carpenters to working again. But not mine—no, sir.

We were going along now, but still we wouldn't have enough money to finish that building. It was going to cost more than had been estimated. And there was the matter of repaying that ten thousand dollars I had borrowed. I went back to the county board. But they wouldn't get us any more funds for Crossnore. Crossnore already had more than the community's share, they said. They wouldn't budge a notch.

So I got on my horse and rode to Morganton, and there I caught the train and went to Raleigh. I went to see the State Superintendent of Public Instruction.

"Dr. Brooks"—he was Dr. E. C. Brooks, later president of North Carolina State College and a grand man in education —"we're building a schoolhouse at Crossnore that we think will be a credit to our mountain section. But we've run out of money. It's costing more than we had figured it would, and I've begged and borrowed about all the funds I can get. I've been trying to get the Avery County school board to give us enough money with which to finish it, but I can't prevail on them to do it. They've given us precious little anyway, and they should do better. I've come over here to see if you can't help me out by talking pretty straight to those men."

I went into details. When I had finished, Dr. Brooks told me that the Avery County superintendent of schools and the county attorney were in Raleigh that day, attending some sort of meeting. He'd seen them.

"Yes," I said, "I know it; I passed them in the hallway on the way to your office."

"Well, Mrs. Sloop," Dr. Brooks said, "you find those men and send them to me; I'll see if I can't make them give you the help you need."

"Thank you," I said, and I started off in search of those two. I figured they'd be in a certain restaurant. I went straight to it, and sure enough, there they sat at a table, eating. I went over to them.

"Gentlemen," I said, "Dr. Brooks would like to see you."

"We've seen him, Mrs. Sloop," one of them said. "We saw him this morning. And thank you."

"But he wants to see you *again*," I said. "I have just this moment come from his office and he asked me to tell you please to come back. He wants to see you, and it's urgent."

I went out. I knew what they were thinking. And thinking about *me*.

But they went to see Dr. Brooks. And, brothers, he laid down the law to those men. Before they left his office, they had agreed to take over that ten thousand dollar debt in the name of Avery County and repay it at the rate of five hundred dollars a year, marked as an appropriation to Crossnore in that amount.

So, after a while and in due season, we finished the big building on the side of the hill.

## 23

MEANWHILE, although we were occupied with getting the schoolhouse built, forty-and-one other things had been happening. Life at Crossnore was on the pioneering order but certainly never dull.

Doctor helped me as much as he could with my various projects, but he had little time he could spare from his medicine. And I tried to help him whenever the opportunity permitted. Often I assisted in operations and handled the office when he was out, which was often, for Doctor seemed constantly to be in the saddle. Many were the long, cold days and the endless nights I waited anxiously for his return. Sometimes I grew nervous and apprehensive, but I never lost my faith in his ability to fight his way home through the worst storms and my trust in a merciful Providence. And he had many frightful experiences.

One dreadful day I particularly remember. Doctor had gone on a long trip, with snow and ice on the roads, across Grassy Ridge into Tennessee. He had told me he would be late getting back, and I soon became awfully uneasy, for a blizzard was coming from that direction and I was afraid of drifts. Drifts are very dangerous in the mountains, where the roads and trails are difficult to follow in deep snow. Doctor's horse could do almost anything, but I didn't know how well she could handle herself in a snowdrift.

Late in the afternoon two boys came from out on Jonas Ridge. They said that a man there who had been a patient of Doctor's was having trouble, that they couldn't relieve the pain caused by his hernia.

There was nothing I could do because I couldn't take the two little children out in that weather. I told them that it was going to be pretty late at night when Doctor got in, and I thought they had better get somebody else if they could. And I wondered where they would try. They had come from about 12 miles away, and Morganton was 25 miles beyond that; but I couldn't do a thing for them.

So they went away, and about nine o'clock they came back and said they couldn't get anybody and that the man was going to die, that everything they knew to do had been done, and they couldn't reduce that hernia.

I made them stay and thaw out, and just before they were getting ready to leave, Doctor came in. I was sorry to hear the horse going down to the barn, because I knew that if Doctor saw those boys he'd go with them. Maybe, I thought, if he didn't see the boys I could soften it up so that he wouldn't go until morning.

But they heard the same noise that I did, for their horses whinnied at Doctor's. Out of the house they flew. And in a little while Doctor came in and said he had changed horses and he guessed he'd go.

He took with him the saddlebags he always carried but nothing at all fitted for a surgical operation. He said he had always been able to reduce that man's hernia, and he felt like he could again. So he went with the boys—after I had fed him.

· Along toward morning he came back, just as cold as a man could be, and said he hadn't walked as much as he usually did on a night like that because he was so tired. That was why he had got so cold; he could generally warm up by walking. He told me that when he got there the man was in bad shape. It meant an immediate operation, else a part of that intestine would have to be removed. But they had nothing but firelight; the kerosene had given out. So with the help of the light from his lantern he undertook that operation. With no aid, boiling the things on the fireplace or the cook stove, he relieved the man, finished up the operation, put on the dressings, and came away.

Nothing was said about money.

The man got well and was much stronger after that than he had been before. He was able to do steady work. But to this day we have never gotten a penny out of it. Yet Doctor still feels, and so do I, that he was paid for doing that operation. He says, because the man got well. I couldn't help thinking that there was just a little bit of the dare in his eyes when he would say to me, even years afterward, "And I did that operation by lantern light with a little scalpel."

It was wonderful the success Doctor—and often Doctor and I together—had with those operations. But then we were operating upon a very sturdy kind of people, a people most of whom had led a clean life and had had practically no tuberculosis and no typhoid fever.

Sometimes in the midst of some particularly serious operation we ourselves would almost lose faith and wonder if that was going to be the one that would ruin our record and make people afraid to be operated upon when they needed it. But they usually got well. They were beginning to appreciate the value of surgery. And by now they no longer suspected that we had settled here just to practice on them and then go somewhere else; they were satisfied that we had come to stay and that our entire purpose and hope was to help them. Confidence grew, and friendships developed and matured.

And then the infant-mortality rate diminished so much, and that was another thing that tied them to our work. The care of the mothers was something so new, and they were so grateful for it.

As the years passed and the willingness to be operated upon increased, we found that there were cases that couldn't wait until warmer weather, and that was when we had begun occasionally to operate in the sickroom. Our custom had been to take everything outdoors, find the best-looking apple tree with the most leaves on it, and set the table underneath. The tree would give us shade that was not so variable. And always the patients took the anesthetic so well because they were out in that good open air—mountain air!

One of the reasons that we liked the outdoors was that it didn't make so much difference about how many people came to see the operation. There was room for them, and we could make them stand back a little more easily.

I didn't realize how many times we had operated under apple trees until one of Doctor's former teachers stopped to see us one day, and he said, "Doctor, they tell me you are doing a good deal of surgery now."

Doctor said, "Yes, we have to."

"Well," he said, "Mrs. Sloop has taken me all around and showed me what you've got, and I haven't seen one thing that looks like an operating room. What do you do?"

Doctor said, "Well, I never have quite made up my mind

yet whether an apple tree is antiseptic or aseptic, but I've never had any infection in an operation I did under an apple tree."

A striking thing that stands out among our experiences as embryo surgeons was the absolute courage of the people. Often it almost amounted to daredevil. One man sent for Doctor to come a tremendous distance up on a mountain. He said he'd seen him operate on other people, and he knew they didn't die. He wanted him to come and operate on him, or so the man who came for him said. Doctor asked, "Well, what's the trouble with him?"

"Oh," he said, "he got shot in the belly last night."

Doctor said, "That's a right serious thing."

"Yes," the man said casually, "and he'll die, too, if he don't get some help."

So Doctor went. For some reason I couldn't go with him. They reached the man's house, and Doctor operated. Every perforation he could find he sewed up, and then he closed up the wound. The man had been shot with a pistol, and the ball had perforated the various folds of the intestine.

After he had finished and was getting ready to go home, Doctor said to him, "Now you must keep exceedingly quiet, for this thing will stand no playing. It will tear; it'll come to pieces if you are not perfectly quiet and if you don't take just what I say as food in your mouth. Don't break any of the rules that I'm giving you."

Then Doctor began to put up his things. And he heard the man in the bed behind him—the patient—say, "Git me my shoes. I've got to go to the spring; I've got to have a drink of water." And he was sitting up on the side of the bed with his feet on the floor!

Again Doctor, having made him lie down, warned him of the danger of moving, told him he must remain quiet. But they said that later that night the man did get up and put on his shoes and go to the spring. And he got well!

139

## 24

DURING most of the time that we were building the new schoolhouse we were also busy at the task of running the school we already had. All the rooms we had available were filled with pupils; we were making excellent use of Treasure Island and the Wart, as well as the more orthodox facilities.

So already we had a high school of sorts, though we were looking forward to completing the big building and having the finest high school in that section of the mountains.

The children from Altamont, along with those in our immediate community, combined to make even at this time a fair-sized high-school group, particularly on days when the weather was good. For that was our Jonah—bad weather. Along with poor transportation.

As the weather got worse, it became more difficult for the pupils to walk to school. An ambitious boy at Altamont, however, did much toward solving that particular problem for the Altamont boys and girls and thereby became in our region the father of consolidation and school-bus transportation. What he did was to persuade his father to let him drive their two-horse team and wagon to Crossnore and back each school day, and in turn I agreed to pay him two dollars a day for the transportation he was providing the children.

But an even more important era for Crossnore was about to begin, and this is how it came about:

One day a girl came to me, a young strip of a girl who looked like she had worked, and worked hard, and said, "Mis' Sloop, I want you to fix a place for me to stay anights. I can't do my work at school and make no progress unless I can stay here. If I stay home, they keep me on Mondays to wash, and they keep me there another day to iron, and they keep another day to help get the wood if it's bad on Sat'day and we can't get wood then. So I can't keep up with my lessons, and I want to stay here anights."

I told her I didn't have a place in the world to put people to sleep.

"Well," she said, "you got your own front porch, and you can let me stay here on the front porch. I'll bring my rations and I'll bring my beddin', and I'll roll it up nice and neat ever' mornin' and put it in the corner, and 'twon't do you no harm."

I told her it was too cold for her to sleep outdoors that way; I couldn't let her do it.

She said, "My attic at home is cold; there ain't nothin' to keep the wind out, and it gets through the cracks. I'm used to it, so I can sleep cold."

The child was determined, I could see, and I wanted so much to help her. Finally I suggested that she go down into the village where a teacher who was married and had a family lived in a little cottage that had an attic to it. She did, and the teacher consented to take her. By the time school opened, she had taken eight girls into that tiny attic! They were sleeping there at night with a great deal of cover which they had brought from home, getting up in the morning and breaking the ice on the water to wash their faces. Then on every Friday afternoon they would go home and on Monday mornings would return with more rations.

Gradually they learned to overcome their timidity and go downstairs and share the kitchen with the teacher—not to cook anything but to heat the food they had brought.

That had gone on a couple of months when the boys came. They were headed by Clarence, a chunky, muscular boy in his late teens, a determined, ambitious fellow with confidence in himself and with unlimited initiative. There were five of these boys who wanted to come from over in the Buck Hill section. If they had come from home each day, they would have had to walk from four to five miles to school, and back. They asked me if I couldn't fix them a place to stay "anights." They said they couldn't come till the crops were all in, but they were about to finish with the crops now. Couldn't I fix them a place like I did for the girls?

The upshot of that was they secured permission from the owner of an old gristmill down in the village to sleep in the attic of this old mill—which was just the same as sleeping out-doors, for there were boarded sides and no strips over the cracks.

The boys brought their straw ticks and straw pillows; if they'd had feathers in them, the rats would eat the ticks and the pillows. The rats in that old gristmill were terrible. They were voracious. The boys had to sleep beside their clothes—they probably had most of them on anyway—and sleep with their food.

One day at school the teacher asked them why they brought a big bundle to school some days and a little bundle other days, for they always brought a bundle. The boys explained that the bundles were their rations, that Monday morning each bundle would be big because they had brought enough from home to last through the week. By Friday morning there wouldn't be much left, and so the bundle would be little. They brought the bundles of food with them to school and hung them on the outside of their desks when they were big and stuck them inside when they had got small. Had they left the food in the attic of the gristmill, the rats would have made short work of it.

Those mill boys endured that winter until the bitter-cold weather came, when they found it very hard to study, for they were not allowed to use anything in the gristmill for light but a kerosene lantern, and they could not study by that. So the teachers in the little teacherage suggested that they come up and study in their kitchen. But when they started studying there, the boys from the village complained that "them mill boys" had a better chance than they did because the teachers would help the mill boys at nights with their lessons.

I said, "Yes, that's their advantage, but your advantage is that you have a warm place to sleep at night and warm food to eat when you go home."

The mill boys turned out some right remarkable men. One of them is now a colonel—a full colonel—in the United States Army. Whenever I get some new word about Clarence and his achievements, I think of him as a young mountain boy living in that old gristmill with the others, and it makes me mighty proud of them all.

The girls living in the attic and the boys living in the old gristmill—that was the beginning of this new and important era, the boarding-school idea that developed into an important part of the Crossnore program. It came out of necessity. Those children just had to have some place to stay in order to go to school, and so a boarding school was the only solution.

The next summer more boys asked to come—from greater distances, too—and they wanted to have something better than the old mill attic. So we decided to build a simple dormitory for them. It was a long building with a partition down the middle and stalls, as it were, on either side, with a door opening out. But it grew slowly, for the money was hard to get. By the time school opened in the fall there was a roof on it, but there was no siding, not even the storm sheeting, no flooring, not even the subfloor. Two of the mill boys— Clarence and Howard—had come from jobs they had elsewhere and worked every spare minute during the summer on that little building.

So when school opened, the boys laid planks over the joists, they set up their beds, they borrowed the stage curtain that we had used the previous commencement, which was made of dark-blue calico, and with it provided for themselves a

143

little protection against the public eye. They built a little outside fireplace nearby and put a tin pan over it because they just had to have warm water for shaving. Practically every boy in that building was old enough to have to shave. They called it the donkey barn, because it did look like a little barn. But it was the beginning of our real dormitories.

The next year we were given money to build one for the girls. It was a little more pretentious. The money with which it was built was given me by the late Mr. Charles Johnston of Charlotte, the textile manufacturer. That building still stands. The old donkey barn later became the dining room—when we decided we must have a dormitory with food furnished—and we built a kitchen onto it.

When school opened after we had built the Johnston Building, everything was so crowded that we decided to use the living room of that building as the Latin-recitation room.

For Uncle Newt was to have his hope fulfilled. We were going to teach Latin.

We calculated that we could seat thirty in that room and that thirty would be far more than would want to take Latin. But they simply swarmed in for high-school work—in all sorts of conveyances. The two-horse wagon wouldn't bring those that lived down toward Linville Falls through Altamont and on up here. So we had to have an imitation school bus made to carry them. They came in from all directions and crowded the little bus beyond its proper capacity. I called it an imitation because it wasn't a regular school bus but a smaller and cheaper model. At first we had used only the two-horse wagon driven by the Altamont boy, as I mentioned. When the wagon could no longer serve, we got an open truck. But in bad weather the children had no protection, and also I was always fearful that someone might fall out. So I went down to the people who made school buses and told them what I needed and explained that money was mighty scarce. They listened, and agreed they'd make us a cheaper bus. So they did. It was on a truck chassis, and it had long seats on the sides, like those at the front of a streetcar. Side curtains were provided that could be put up on rainy or cold days.

"We called the bus we were building for Crossnore School the 'Mis' Sloop's Body,'" the man told me. "And when the people from other schools came to see us about making them some buses, I showed 'em the 'Mis' Sloop's Body,' and they ordered us to make them some as quick as we could. Which we did. And that's the name we gave those buses."

So we got "Mis' Sloop's Body" and began transporting the children to and from school. But we found out quickly that there were more pupils than we had thought there would be, although we had expected a large attendance.

I was very much interested in what was going to happen in the Latin room. I had prophesied that there would be a good-sized group taking Latin. The teachers wouldn't agree. They were college-bred women, and they knew that children in high school didn't take Latin of their own choice. But I guessed there'd be as many as fifteen who'd want it.

Soon after school opened that first morning, a child came down from the Latin-recitation room—the improvised one— and said to me, "Mis' Sloops, Teacher says please come on up there. She can't do nothin' with 'em."

I thought, of course, that the big boys were of a mind that this little college-bred city girl couldn't make them behave and so she was having trouble with them. When I got there, I found that the room was crowded and they were standing on the steps outside. She looked perfectly helpless as she faced me from the other end of the room.

"What's the trouble?" I asked.

"Mrs. Sloop," she said, "you told me that I wouldn't have more than fifteen pupils, and now I've counted thirty-five and I can't seat them all in this room. How can I teach Latin?"

"Oh, well," I said, "some of them just can't take Latin."

"Yes, ma'am, we can too. You promised us Latin," they said, protestingly, "and we're agoin' to take Latin."

So we brought in all sorts of benches and chairs and set them against the wall and finally crowded in the whole thirty-five—and we had our first big Latin class.

We gave them the full high-school Latin course. But when the high school grew still more and we didn't have enough teachers to assign four periods to Latin, the principal, who had been teaching in a high school in Canonsburg, Pennsylvania, and knew the modern trend in regard to Latin, suggested that they cut out the last two years and use it for some other subject. He told me one afternoon that he was nearly mobbed that morning at chapel when he made the announcement that the last two years of Latin were being dropped. He said they came up to him after chapel and said, "She promised us four years of Latin. She said that she keeps her promise." They always called me "she."

"What did you do?" I asked him.

"I argued awhile, and then I gave them four years of Latin," he said.

We still teach Latin at Crossnore, though they have had to accept two years instead of four—and that's two years more than a lot of modern schools offer, I'm sorry to say.

The love of Latin is not only taught them by their relatives in the old country, but it was also handed down to the people of the mountains by Uncle John Wise.

Uncle John was one of three brothers. He was the oldest, Uncle Newt (he was not the Uncle Newt who asked me if we were going to teach Latin in the new school; he was Uncle Newt Clark) was next, and Uncle Tom was the youngest.

These three men had been raised in the low country—below the mountains, as they expressed it—and were naturally Confederates and joined the Confederate Army, while the men in the mountains were nearly all Union men. To the mountain men it was somebody fighting against the flag, and their ancestors had given their lives and their blood to preserve the Union. So they were not going to join anybody who was fighting against the flag.

But Uncle John, Uncle Newt, and Uncle Tom were very faithful Confederates, and though they had moved into this country and were very much alone in that respect, they went every year regularly on horseback to some place where they could take a train and go to the Confederate veterans' reunion. Their pictures were often taken together and they were called the Three Wise Men.

Uncle John was very anxious that the children in this isolated section of the country should have an education. So he began teaching school, way back before the turn of the century, and he taught for many years. The parents of his school children paid him for teaching, of course, though precious little. He said he felt that he must have at least ten dollars a month income and he liked to make it twenty so he could send more to the old 'oman, as he called his wife, who stayed at home and kept the children. He went from place to place throughout the year, teaching at six schools with a period of two months to each.

I said to him one day, "Uncle John, how did you grade your schools and how did you graduate your pupils, if you had only two months a year at each school?"

"I never graded 'em, and I never graduated 'em," he said, pounding with his fist on the table, "but I never let 'em quit till they could read Caesar."

Then I asked, "Uncle John, why were your own children not able to read and write if you taught school all the time? It seems to me they'd be the first ones you'd teach."

"We lived so far off there weren't no chance to get together enough for a school there, and I just couldn't afford to give up the time to teach my own young 'uns. The people were so anxious to have their schools, and I just kept on teachin' six schools a year, and mine just got no learnin'."

His own children, old people now, are living here in this part of the country, and they can't read or write. Yet Uncle John taught Caesar.

## 25

LOOKING back, I believe I'd say that those busy years, that period preceding, during, and immediately following World War I, were perhaps the years of greatest accomplishment at Crossnore. We have done more, of course, in the years since. We have built our school from that old planked-up log structure into the present twenty-five-building institution since 1911, and by far the greatest growth has been in the recent years. But in this period centering around World War I we put the train on the track and got ready to make our run.

That was the time of great enthusiasm. And enthusiasm for something always brings accomplishment. The citizens around Crossnore began to catch fire, early in that prewar period. They saw a vision, and they worked to make the vision real. Those were great days. I shall never forget them. But oh, the heartaches, too, the disappointments, the misunderstandings!

Well do I remember how in the midst of this quickening, this warming for better education and greater opportunities, there suddenly appeared a strange coolness, a slackening of interest, a lethargy. I couldn't understand it; it seemed so strange. So I went to a friend and asked frankly what had brought about this new attitude.

"The word's agoin' around that the Presbyterians is afixin' to take over the school and run it as a Presbyterian school," my friend said.

I was amazed. Something had to be done. I thought and thought.

People in the mountains have great respect for law. Let the law say that Crossnore would be no Presbyterian or Baptist or Methodist or any other sort of denominational school. Let it be put down in the law that Crossnore School was and always would be a public school.

Then I hit it. We'd incorporate the school. We'd get a charter.

And that's what we did. We proceeded to draw up a legal paper in the form of a charter upon which the seal of the state of North Carolina would be affixed. This charter provided that no denomination would ever own or control Crossnore School, Inc., but on the contrary it would have a board of trustees that would direct its operation and would have authority to buy and sell property. But, though nondenominational, Crossnore would be interested in the spreading of the Christian religion and making it more vital in our community and the homes Crossnore would touch.

I'll never forget the meeting we had to read the charter. It was on an utterly cold afternoon, with wind and sleet making it even worse. But everybody came. The charter was read, sentence by sentence, slowly and with full discussion of every point. And when the document had been drawn to satisfy everybody, it was adopted and trustees were elected. That was when Uncle Alex was named our first trustee. I remember, too, it was then that we decided to add more rooms to the little schoolhouse in order to be able more effectively to teach home economics and manual training.

Chartering the school restored the community's enthusiasm, and we went to work again. That meeting was one of the high lights of the period. A nasty rumor had almost stopped our forward progress, but we had stifled it.

Nor will I ever forget another meeting that came some time later, but still in that early era of Crossnore School. It was soon after I had got myself appointed attendance officer and had proceeded to enforce the compulsory-attendance law.

I had been having trouble with a number of the parents. The law in Avery County required children to attend school until they were seventeen. And that was rather old, many patrons felt. Nor did they agree that anybody had a right to tell them when they could keep their children at home. They thought that was a question to be settled in their own homes and nobody had any right to invade their premises.

The mountain people have a strong feeling for the rights of the individual. It's a heritage, no doubt, from their English ancestry. They don't think—and certainly they didn't in those days—that anyone has a right to come between them and their children.

So, frequently they kept their children at home to do work or for some other reason they considered good. It was giving me much trouble. I had the children on my side; they were eager to come to school, almost all of them. I told them they must help me in my efforts to help them attend school regularly; I explained that they must help us educate their parents to the value of regular school attendance. And I suggested how they might do this.

First, I said, they were to beg not to be kept home to dig potatoes or pick beans. The parents had time to do this, but time-honored custom decreed that it was a job for the children. Second, if they begged to no avail and had to stay at home, then they were to cry—not a little soft sob, but a loud, heartrending wail. This second method, I found, often worked. Parents were so proud of children who wanted that badly to go to school that they would relent and dig the potatoes and pick the beans themselves. Or else they just couldn't stand the noise and let their dear offspring go to school in order to have some peace and quiet.

But if neither of these plans worked, I told the children just to pout. They were to do the work their parents decreed, of course, but were not to do it pleasantly; they were to go about it unsmiling and glum, with the air of injured inno-

150

cence, the attitude of martyrdom. That almost always worked. The parents sent them back to school in self-defense.

But sometimes nothing was successful. The parents simply refused to obey the compulsory-school-attendance law. Teachers and I argued with them to no avail. They insisted on the right of "home rule." They wanted their children educated, they said, but not emancipated. And now, they told me, I was not doing them right; I said I had come to help them educate their children, and they supposed I had, but now I was seeking to take away their authority over their own children. They just wouldn't obey any law that did that to them; they didn't believe there was such a law anyway.

So I was forced to have them arrested. And the time came for the trials.

That's the meeting I said I'd never forget. Sixteen angry, defiant parents had been summoned, and everyone was there. I would have given years of my life not to have been forced to face them that day. The room was filled. They were accustomed to trials; I was not. They had been to see lawyers, they said, who had told them there was no such law. They confronted me with blazing eyes.

Their spokesman arose, presented their case, argued fervently that parents had authority over their children and that no one could tell them not to keep them home when they were needed at home, said that any law requiring such a thing would be an unreasonable law, and (to cap the climax) declared that there was no such law on the books. He spoke sincerely, in the fashion of the mountain man, and convincingly.

And now those angry eyes were turned once again upon me. What was I to say? What could I do? How could I show them that I hadn't been trying to trick them? How prove I hadn't lied?

I said nothing. I simply opened my bag, took out the law book, opened it to the page. I handed it, my finger pointing

151

out the section, to the man who had just finished speaking, and asked him to read it.

Right here I want once more to testify to the inherent honesty, the high principles, of the people of the mountains, for never have I seen their nobility better demonstrated than at this meeting.

The man looked first at the outside cover of the book, then at the title page. And then he began reading the law. He read slowly, carefully, through the entire section. He closed the book, handed it to me.

"She's right," he said.

Not a protest was raised, not another angry word voiced. I began talking with them; I made an appeal for their cooperation; I told them we wanted a good school and I knew they wanted it too, and I explained that we could not have such a school unless we maintained an excellent attendance. The law was reasonable and for the good of the children. Then the teacher spoke, explaining the necessity for regular attendance, for day-by-day presence at school of the pupil, of every pupil who could possibly come, in order to keep the school going forward.

They listened to us quietly and most attentively, and when we had finished they promised, quietly too and without any dramatics, that never again would they be guilty of violating that law.

And I wish to say that these sixteen never did—not once. You can depend upon the people of the mountains when they give their word.

## 26

AT the outset of our program of development at Crossnore, a most fortunate thing happened for us. It was the visit to our campus of a young girl from Illinois. That visit is still paying dividends.

The girl was Betty Bailey, the daughter of a professor at the University of Illinois who was then head of that university's geology department. At the end of her junior year —it was 1920 or maybe the next year—her father came into this country to make some investigations among the various mines of this section, for our country is rock-ribbed with valuable minerals. He brought Betty with him, and they were staying at the little hotel in Pineola. They had found a particular interest in that hotel because all the woodwork— window casings, doors, and door frames—were made of black walnut. Walnut was plentiful in this country. The people valued it, and so they had used it to trim—as they expressed it—their first hotel.

One morning at this hotel Betty had met someone who knew me and who was coming over to Crossnore to see what was happening at the school. They walked the three miles that morning, though the road from Pineola to Crossnore in those days was very rough. I showed them about the school grounds, took them over the new big building on the hill, and told them of our plans for other buildings.

"Mrs. Sloop," Betty asked me, as we walked, "would there be any chance in the world for me to teach at Crossnore?"

"Have you graduated from college?" I asked her.

"No," she said, "and I can't stop school until I do, but by next year I will be a graduate, and then I want to come to Crossnore to teach."

Next year she came. She was the beginning of a series of college graduates, young women from the big colleges of the country, who came here and built up and established standards of education for our school that we never could have had otherwise.

It was not long after she had arrived at Crossnore and begun to teach that she asked me a question. And that question was one of the most fortunate things that ever happened for us, I must say.

153

"Mrs. Sloop," she said to me one day, "why don't you get help for your school from the DAR?"

I had joined the DAR about the turn of the century, and this fact perhaps had heightened my interest in the stories told of Revolutionary times and Revolutionary soldiers in the mountain region. I had begun to ask the old men of our section questions related to the Revolutionary period, and I made a habit of taking along with me a notebook in which I jotted down what they said and listed the names of Revolutionary soldiers and their children and grandchildren.

Betty's question set me to thinking. I in turn questioned her about her interest in the DAR. I learned that she was regent of her home chapter. Some time after our conversation she served as a page at the DAR Congress in Washington. There she presented the cause of Crossnore so effectively that she was told that I might come and ask that the school be put on the approved-schools list. I did. That was about 1924. Crossnore was added to the DAR's list of approved schools, and that has meant a great deal to us. Crossnore is not a school to which the DAR contributes directly; but it sanctions Crossnore, and many DAR chapters and larger groups as well as individual DAR members have contributed liberally and most effectively. Without the help of the DARs we would never have been able to expand our facilities as we have done, and we could never have served the boys and girls of our mountain section to the extent that we have in the three decades since Betty Bailey hit upon that wonderful idea.

We became much interested in the DAR, of course, and that made us want a chapter here at Crossnore. We began to look up old records and get affidavits concerning Revolutionary lines, until we had twelve members, one or two of them teachers. I was a member, as was Uncle Newt's daughter, and there were others like her who were descended from Revolutionary soldiers who had fought at King's Mountain. The papers were accepted, and we organized our chapter.

Since that time we have done a lot of work in looking up family lines and genealogies, and I must say it is a fascinating pursuit.

Our DAR activities, in fact, have aroused a great deal of interest in ancestry, and the people are very grateful for the work that has been done in obtaining authentic information, in marking the graves of Revolutionary soldiers, which we are still doing, and in interesting the younger people in learning about the type of ancestors they had.

Uncle John Wise was one of my best historians—my very best, in fact—but several others were also good historians and supplied me with many interesting facts.

The battle of King's Mountain—which, on October 7, 1780, broke the backbone of the British campaign in the South and led the way to the final triumph of the American cause at Yorktown—was our finest field of research. In those desperate days the men volunteered as fast as they could join General Sevier and take part in the fighting, and virtually all of them were in that decisive battle.

Uncle Billy Davis was probably the veteran of King's Mountain who lived the longest. He lived to be a hundred and fourteen years old, in spite of the fact that he had been seriously wounded in the thigh. He was given first aid on the battlefield, though it must have been of the crudest kind, and came on home to spend the rest of his life with a sore leg, one that was always painful and of very little use, and for years before he died he simply sat with it in its terrible condition of infection.

Uncle Tom Wise told me that as a six-year-old boy he once went with his mother to see old Uncle Billy. She held him by the hand, he said, and warned him that he must be real quiet because Uncle Billy was always sick. When they went in, his mother said, "Well, how is Uncle Billy today?"

"Oh," he answered, "I'm just fine, fine. They're agoin' to have to shoot the old soldier yet before they get rid of him."

Uncle Tom told me that he'd never in the world forget that visit, for that leg smelled awful and looked awful. The flies were crawling all over it. They knew nothing of antiseptics. They had nothing to take care of it with. He just endured it and was cheerful to the end—of a hundred and fourteen years!

Later on in my efforts to develop our DAR chapter I went to see Uncle Thad Braswell, who at that time was ninety-four years of age and who was supposed to have known some Revolutionary soldiers.

Uncle Thad was in a pretty bad humor that morning. But he was willing to talk. I asked him to let me see the Braswell family Bible, which had been so much quoted to me and referred to by Braswell descendants.

"I ain't got it," he said.

"Where is it, Uncle Thad?" I asked him.

"It's burnt up," he said.

"Uncle Thad, how did it get burnt up? Did your house burn down?"

"No," he answered. "I throwed it in the fire."

"Why, Uncle Thad, that was a very valuable book."

"That's what they tell me," he said. "But they brought too many young 'uns around here, and they got ahold o' that book one day and played with it and got it all tore up, and I just picked it up and throwed it in the fire."

Now, remember, Uncle Thad was old. Men of ninety-four have to be allowed their tantrums.

I said, "Uncle Thad, maybe you could tell me a good deal that I want to know. Didn't you used to know some of the old Revolutionary soldiers?"

"Yes," he said, "I knowed a lot of 'em and their wives, too. I mind one of them used to go to church with his wife all the time—the same church I went to—and that was the whitest woman I ever saw. She never looked like she had a drop of blood in her body. But she could walk to church just

156

the same. I guess she had the same stuff in her her old husband had, 'cause they said he was a mighty good soldier.

"But," he added, "if you want women descendants of Revolutionary soldiers, all you got to do is to go hunt up Billy Davis and his young 'uns. Half the women in Avery County is descended from Billy Davis."

Then I said, "Uncle Thad, the only mistake you make there is that two-thirds of them, and maybe three-fourths, are descended from Billy Davis." And that is true.

"But," I asked him, "why is it that we don't have any Davises scarcely at all in this county? You'd think there'd have been as many men of that name as women."

"No," he said, "there weren't but three of the boys, and they were an ornery lot. They never stayed in this county. They moved out."

To Uncle Thad their moving away was proof that the men were ornery. The women stayed, so they were all right.

From others we also received information that helped us in tracing satisfactorily the ancestral lines of women of our mountain region who wished to join our chapter. And few there are indeed in the mountains who are not eligible.

Nor would I attempt to evaluate the work the DAR has done for Crossnore except to say that we are deeply indebted to this patriotic organization of women of America and to countless individuals within it, many of whom are among my most beloved friends. Much of this work has been in the realm of the spirit, I'd say, in inspiration given us and enthusiasm to broaden our undertakings and strive harder to accomplish them. But much too has been done in the very practical realm of the material—in bricks and mortar and cement blocks and timbers.

Not many years after we attained the distinction of being admitted to the DAR list of approved schools, the North Carolina Daughters of the American Revolution built our Big Girls' dormitory. Mrs. Ralph Van Landingham of Charlotte was one of our enthusiastic supporters, and the money for this project was raised during her term as state chairman of approved schools.

The C. W. Johnston Building had been built to house thirty girls, and already eighty-four were living in it. It was simply overflowing. So we moved the big girls into the new North Carolina DAR building, and it was about that time that I remember—and to this day I am thrilled at recalling it—being handed a telegram from Mrs. Van Landingham saying that Mrs. Gregory Graham of Winston-Salem had contributed enough money to build a dormitory for the little girls in memory of her mother.

So we can happily give our best bow to the DAR ladies and list some of their major contributions toward the development of our campus—its material development: the two buildings already named, given by the North Carolina DAR and Mrs. Graham; the contributions from DAR women of the nation to the construction of the administration building, including a ten thousand dollar legacy provided by the late Mrs. W. N. Reynolds of Winston-Salem; the music building, given to Crossnore by the Junior DAR; and the new Middle Girls' dormitory, on one of the prettiest sites on the campus, whose cost was provided in the main by the North Carolina DARs and by them has been named the Mary Martin Sloop Building. In a conspicuous position on one of the walls of the main lounge of this new building, the finest on the campus, the dear ladies have hung a new oil portrait of me, a handsome work—work, not subject, mind you—by Mr. Charles Tucker of Charlotte and Rock Hill, South Carolina, the well-known Carolina artist.

This portrait was presented at the 1952 commencement exercises, with my friend, Mrs. Preston B. Wilkes of Charlotte, doing the presenting and my son-in-law, Mr. Dwight Fink, the high-school principal, accepting it on my behalf. I was sick in bed at the time—one of the few times I've ever had to miss anything big—but I found out everything that was said and done. And was I proud! I must admit it. I was delighted at having received the portrait to hang in the building—but I was as proud as a peacock at having had this beautiful and highly useful building named for me.

27

IT was during this period of the middle twenties that we undertook another heavy task—one that was burdensome to us, though it was also greatly rewarding.

That was the building of our Presbyterian church, a structure of which we are especially proud. Many visitors have warmly admired it and have told us that nowhere have they seen a more interesting and unique sanctuary.

Uncle Will Franklin built it. I have already introduced Uncle Will. He was the old gentleman who some years before had expressed his commiseration for me because Uncle Elias had given me such a financial beating in selling me the land on which much of Crossnore was later to be built—a deal that soon turned into one of the best I've ever made. He was a carpenter and stonemason, operated a sawmill and tannery, and was quite a character. I shall never forget Uncle Will.

Uncle Will had thirteen children. He lived up at the head of Bill White Creek and Hoot Owl Hollow. Never was there a more promising bunch of children than Uncle Will's. The wife was as faithful a mother as ever lived, and anxious to have her children educated.

But Uncle Will couldn't read or write, and he saw little use in schooling. As the lumber business picked up, Uncle Will became more able to do things for his family. And he began letting them go to Berea College out in Kentucky. He wouldn't help them with any money; he thought it was enough if he did without their work.

It was after Uncle Will's children had scattered—in the middle twenties—that we determined to build a church. Some neighbors had asked for a Presbyterian Sunday school, and they wanted a Presbyterian church. Years before, the Baptists had built a church with free lumber and free labor. It had done a world of good in the community. But these people were Presbyterians, and they wanted a Presbyterian church. After using a little three-hundred-dollar chapel for a while and then selling it in 1926 to be made into a residence, we actually began the big rock church which now stands at Crossnore—and will stand for many years. And the story of the church is also the story of Uncle Will.

He was a wonderful builder, and we wanted him to undertake building the church. But when he was asked to do it, he shook his head. "No," he said, "I'll not do it."

But he was the only man, we thought, who could undertake such a task, for he was especially good in rock building, and we wanted a church made of rock hauled out of the river. So I approached him myself and asked him to build the church, but he refused flatly. We kept after him, though, with great persistence. Finally one day as he passed by my house I called to him, and I said, "Uncle Will, if you don't do like I ask you, something's going to happen to you. You've got a chance now to build a church, and that's a good thing for a man to do; and you're refusing to do it."

He said, "I ain't agoin' to live so much longer; I'm seventy years old, and if I build all the houses my young 'uns want me to build for them, I'll be ready to take a long journey."

I said, "Uncle Will, if you don't watch out, that journey's going to end in the wrong direction."

"Aw," he said, "I ain't ascared o' you nor the Devil neither." On he walked. And it was true. Uncle Will just didn't scare easily.

But finally he was persuaded to build the church. And it was in this way:

160

He had begun coming to church occasionally in the little chapel. I suggested to the building committee of the church that they go over to Uncle Will's home the first thing after church the next Sunday morning and ask him formally to build that church, that they felt that he was the only person to do it.

So the building committee promised to go immediately after church up Bill White Creek to Uncle Will's house in Hoot Owl Hollow and put the proposition to him.

But when we walked into Sunday school that next morning, there sat Uncle Will on the front seat. He had come to church, and he aimed to hear all that was said. When the service was over, I said to the men, "Go on out now before Uncle Will gets away. The women and I are going to have our prayer circle while you all are talking with him, and we'll pray that he'll say yes."

We women prayed, and when I came out after the prayer meeting, I saw Uncle Will leaning against a tree not far from the chapel. I called to him and said, "Uncle Will, I'm so glad you have decided to build our church."

He looked up, and he said, "Hunnhh! I'd like to know how you know what I have decided."

"Oh," I said, "a little bird told me about it. I'm up here among the birds." The steps to the church were high, and he was downhill.

He said, "Well, I guess I'll try it." And he did. It's just amazing how a man will change his mind sometimes.

A man brought his two horses and wagon, and every day he hauled rocks from down at the bank of the river up a steep hill a mile or more to the site of the church, until he had brought up enough rocks to make all the walls of that church. And they were thick, solid walls. There is no framework for it.

Uncle Will would not have more than four workmen at a time. He had his own peculiar way of keeping books, and he

161

generally hired boys whom he could boss. But no boys were able to do the rock laying for that beautiful church, and so he hired an older man to help him to lay the rock while the boys did the rest.

He kept his records in a little notebook. He brought it to me every two weeks for me to pay off the men for building the church. One day I said, "Why don't you pay the boys every week? It's so much better for them."

" 'Tain't neither," he said. "Let 'em learn to take care o' their money and not spend it all every week."

In that book he kept a record of every day's work. It consisted of a series of figures across a page—9, 9½, 9, 10, 9½, and so forth—and I said, "Uncle Will, what does this mean?"

"Add 'em up," he said, "and they make the number of hours they worked during the two weeks." I did. And Uncle Will knew exactly what it was going to be.

I said, "What are you paying them this week?" For he paid them according to the work they did and according to their grade of work.

Then he'd say, "Well, this boy don't need but twelve and a half cents an hour this week; he loafed a good deal. This one, yes, he made fifteen cents this week; he's a smart boy." And on it went. He never had a regular set of prices for their work. When I'd add it all up, I'd write the checks, and Uncle Will knew exactly what each check was to be.

So Uncle Will worked on the new church. But when the walls were finished one day, he took his tools and went home. We went to see what was the matter that he wouldn't come to work, and he said, "Them blueprints said to make a barn roof, and them walls is too good to put a barn roof on 'em, and I ain't agoin' to do it. When you let me put on a roof like I want, I'll finish it."

I explained to the men that what he meant was that it was to be a vaulted roof and he had never seen a church with a vaulted roof. So I told them to take Uncle Will over to Blow-

162

ing Rock and show him the two churches there that had vaulted roofs. He wanted an inside ceiling.

They did. And Uncle Will took quite a fancy to the beautiful big timbers that composed the frameworks of those roofs. They were English-type buildings.

So he came back home, and we sent over to see if he was going to go on with the building. His wife said that he had gone up into the woods with one of the boys and a saw and an ax, but she didn't know what he was getting timber for. But it turned out to be the timbers for the church—and they were beautiful timbers when finished—at least 35 feet long.

He hauled them over to the church, and came by to see me and said, "Now I got the timbers for that roof, and I aim to build it. But you'll have to write to Win and tell him to come up here and help me frame that roof; there ain't nobody here knows how to do it."

I said, "Uncle Will, we can't hire Win." (Win was one of his seven sons; Winfred was his name.) "He's been to Berea, he has learned good carpentry, he's in Florida now as a contractor and with large contracts for building, and he couldn't afford to work for the little bit we could pay."

"You write and tell Win," he said, "that I said to git on the first bus that comes up here, and I'll pay him a dollar and a half a day while he works, and our day is ten hours long and if we don't git through then we go longer."

I sat down and wrote Win exactly what he said, but I never expected him to come. But Win did come—on the first bus. I told him of my surprise.

"Mrs. Sloop," he said, "I've been doing what Pappy says a lot longer than you might think, and I aim to keep on doing it."

So the church was built, and it is a beautiful one. And it was built according to Uncle Will's ideas, for none of the rest of us could conceive of the beauty of that structure. When it came to the pulpit, he had his own ideas about how that pulpit was to look. The platform was built up of rock all around, and then a certain type of wooden floor was put on top. The pulpit was built entirely too high, for Uncle Will was over six feet. I protested, but he said that the preacher could get a stool if he didn't like it; he was building it for tall people.

Into that pulpit, built of small stones and in the most artistic way, Uncle Will incorporated a metal slab that he had bent to look like an open book. He said, "I don't know much about the Bible, but it seems to me there ought to be an open book around the pulpit. So I just put one in."

He was always pleased with himself when he thought of something original like that.

In the same way on the two posts for flowers—one on either side of the pulpit—he had made the top flat and into the cement had stuck twelve little round stones. He said, "I hear my wife ateachin' our young 'uns about the twelve tribes of Israel, and I just thought I'd put twelve stones in here to represent the twelve tribes of Israel she reads to 'em about."

Then the pulpit seat was to be built. And when it was done, it was a beautiful thing.

But it didn't quite suit the preacher. He suggested a change. And when he left, Uncle Will put up his tools and said to the boy who was helping him, "Well, William, he thinks he can build it better than we can; let's let him try it."

And off went Uncle Will. It took a number of visits out to his house to get him back to build the seat just as he wanted to build it.

He said to me one day, "I can put some hooks in the back here between these rocks to hang a padding on because the preacher says the rocks will hurt his back."

I said, "You're not going to do it, Uncle Will. We're not going to cover that pretty rockwork up with cushions. If it hurts his back, tell him to send me his Sunday vest and I'll pad it so the rocks won't hurt. But that seat is going to stay

164

The "Donkey Barn," the first single-room dormitory for twenty-two boys (*above*). The boys about to go to work on the foundation for their new dormitory, 1950 (*below*).

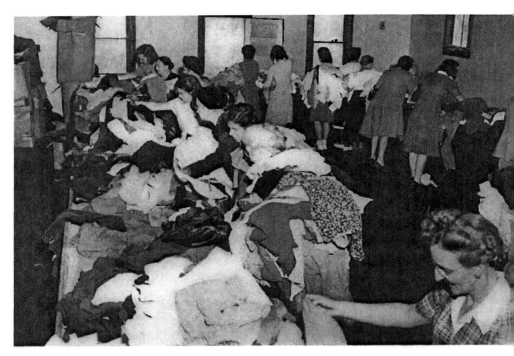

(*above*) Not Macy's on sale day but Uncle Gilmer's and Aunt Pop's Old Clothes Store. (*below, left*) Uncle Gilmer and Aunt Pop, Crossnore's most successful merchants. (*below, right*) The barter system: food is delivered at the kitchen in exchange for old clothes.

just as it is." And it did. Many artists, in the years since it was built, have told us that it is a piece of real art.

In fact, we think that the entire building, inside and out, is distinctive. The handsome rockwork always draws the compliments of visitors, and the high-vaulted interior, with the crossed beams of huge pine timbers, gives our little mountain church almost the appearance of a cathedral. The church really is more Episcopalian in design and general feeling, particularly on the inside, than it is Presbyterian.

So Uncle Will packed up his tools and left, and we had our church. In the years since he built it, Uncle Will and others who worked on it have passed on, but they left their monument in a beautiful structure that has been of great value to our community.

Uncle Will's church has been used. From its pulpit the Good News has been proclaimed regularly, and we will never be able to measure the effect of that preaching. Nor can we know what will be the full fruit of our Sunday-school activities. Doctor, by the way, for years has been the adult Bible-school teacher and this assignment has brought him much pleasure. More and more we emphasize the value of religious training at Crossnore, and we feel that no other training is as important. This nation, we are convinced, must have a spiritual awakening if it is to endure. So we seek to interest our pupils in the things of the spirit. Many of them regularly attend the Presbyterian church. Others go to the other churches in the community.

For Crossnore is well blessed with churches. They occupy, literally as well as figuratively, commanding places in our community. The Presbyterian church that Uncle Will built, for instance, is at the top of one of the highest hills. You can drive up, or walk if you have the time, from the highway far below. Or you can cross over the highway on a wooden bridge and trudge along the steep path that goes straight up to the front door of the church. That's the way we usually go, even though it's strenuous walking for a stout couple well past their threescore years and ten.

It's the same way if you want to go to the Baptist church at Crossnore. It sits right on the edge of the circular flat in the heart of the village. But at that point the land rises steeply, so that to reach the church you must climb seventy-two steps. I know there are that many, because many a time I have counted them.

"What makes you build your churches on such high places?" a visitor asked me one day.

"Religion comes high in Crossnore," I answered. "There isn't but one church in Crossnore on the level, and that's the Methodist. And they wouldn't build their church on a high place because they were afraid they'd fall from grace."

That's a standard Crossnore joke. I guess you can tell I didn't just make it up.

## 28

THINKING back upon those days when we built the church overlooking the little circle of level land where old George Crossnore ran his store, I recall with deep affection another building.

It was one of the first we built as we started up the slope on which Crossnore School was to take root and grow. By all architectural standards, or lack of them, it was a queer structure. And as time went along and we enlarged it or otherwise changed it, that small building got even queerer-looking.

We called it the little teacherage. It was a small frame cottage. Its principal distinction, if it could be said to have any distinction, was its large dining room and the fact that although it housed five teachers, it had not a single bedroom. There were also a kitchen, a living room, and a dressing room.

The teachers slept on a large upstairs porch that in winter certainly provided full benefit of fresh mountain air.

I shall never forget those five teachers. They were all college-bred women, excellent teachers, too. I wonder what present-day teachers would think of the salaries those women received. I distinctly remember that during the two years she was with us the primary teacher was paid by Avery County the magnificent salary of seventeen dollars a month! But the principal did even better; she got forty-two dollars! Of course, it wasn't quite that bad, because thirty-odd years ago a dollar would buy something, and the neighbors brought in vegetables and often meat, and I paid the bills for such groceries as sugar and coffee and other things the people didn't raise.

I want to say a word about the principal. She brought something new to Crossnore. She was the woman who taught Crossnore how to play baseball! It may sound incredible, but when we came to Crossnore they didn't play baseball up here, nor football nor basketball, either. They pitched horseshoes and ran foot races and broad-jumped and high-jumped, and wrestled, and did other sports that we now generally classify under the category of track events. And they played children's games! Yes, even the big boys and the grown men. They played games that are now considered exclusively children's games, such as base and fox and geese.

I'll never forget the sorrow that overspread our little community when a grown man with a family, one of whose granddaughters is now a leading patron of our school and a beloved member of the Crossnore community, broke his neck playing fox and geese. These men were chasing each other, just as children do in playing this game, when this man jumped a branch to get away from his pursuers. In some way he lost his footing, and his head struck a stump, breaking his neck and killing him almost instantly.

But I was telling about the woman principal who introduced baseball to Crossnore, a happier subject! I doubt if any of the children had ever even seen a game. This woman was a marvelous player, but she was even better as a coach. She worked with the children, and she got up an excellent team, considering the fact that none of the members had known even the rudiments of the game. Naturally, that made her one of the most popular teachers in school.

Later we got a Davidson College graduate as a teacher, and he took over the baseball coaching. They played the first regular game in a cow pasture near the campus. This young man helped the boys get an old truck, on which they carried the team to the railroad station where they could catch the train to take them off to play some other school's team. Often the old truck would break down, or they couldn't get the engine started, and they'd have to push it, maybe for miles. Once, I recall, they had to push it a long way up a steep hill. I suppose that helped, though—helped supply the muscle to knock many a home run!

But I want to finish my story of the little teacherage. About the beginning of the twenties we enlarged it to accommodate eight teachers. But even then it still had not one bedroom. Some time later we put up a tent beside the little teacherage, and two teachers slept in it. The tent likewise was thoroughly air-conditioned.

Before I get away from the little teacherage, I want to tell of an incident that happened there. Maybe I shouldn't tell it, because it doesn't reflect much credit on Crossnore School. But I'm going to anyway; I think it amusing, especially as I look back upon it after all these years.

They had a copper boiler out in the yard at the teacherage. I think they used it for washing clothes. At any rate, it was there and it was made of copper. Now, as everybody in the mountains knows, copper is the perfect material for corn-liquor stills.

One day this copper boiler disappeared. Some time after

that we were quite sure that several of the older boys in the school were showing signs of being tipsy. And it wasn't long until one day one of the men at the school came to me and said, "Mrs. Sloop, you remember that copper boiler that disappeared from the teacherage?"

I said I did.

"Well," he said, "I've found it. And you'd never guess where. Some of our big boys stole it and set it up on the ravine branch and have been amakin' a run of liquor. Yes, ma'am, that's where your copper boiler went."

Those rascals had rigged up that boiler as a still not more than a couple of hundred yards—maybe not that far—from my office and were actually making liquor right under my nose!

Well, they didn't make any more—in that boiler and on that branch—not on the Crossnore campus, at any rate.

The old teacherage became our first dining room and kitchen—after the teachers had moved to the new teacherage. We were great on improvising at Crossnore—and we still have to do it from time to time.

In 1922 our first high-school class was graduated from our new high-school building on the hill. It was our smallest class —only two pupils—but we were so proud of it! One of these was Gurney Franklin. For a long while, several years as I remember, he had walked each day seven miles to school and seven miles home. The other graduate was Nell Johnson, one of Uncle Alex's daughters, who had to walk two miles each day in order to complete her high-school course.

Another thing I remember quite well, though it has been three decades since we did it. That was the fact that Crossnore High School led the entire state of North Carolina in percentage of attendance. Our thirty-five students, though many of them lived miles from the school and though the weather was often fearful, established a record of 96.3 per cent average daily attendance. I'll never forget that figure. We

169

beat Durham, which never before had been beaten. And that year we had the distinction of having Dr. J. Y. Joyner, the State Superintendent of Public Instruction, come from Raleigh to deliver our commencement address.

At this time a serious housing problem still remained. The twenty-two little boys were crowded into one big room that had been a shop. It was too small for twenty-two children. We had double-decker beds rather wider than the usual ones that we'd gotten from World War I, and in some of these double-deckers there were three little ones sleeping on the bottom deck and two on the top.

It was too crowded; we knew that. But they had wanted to come to Crossnore, and their folks had wanted them to come. We had for them a wonderful housemother who had been raised right here in the mountains.

But all the time we talked to them and they talked to us about a new dormitory.

We began to try to save up money for it, but it came in so slowly. One spring afternoon a little boy said, "Mis' Sloop, we ain't never agoin' to get our new dormitory."

I said, "Oh, yes, we are. And we're going to begin work on it right now." I suggested that he go and get the boys out and collect some tools and meet me in a little while up on the side of the hill where we were going to build the new dormitory.

He did. And those little chaps from six to twelve years of age spent two hours of real work clearing off the underbrush, digging up the little roots, and getting ready for the new dormitory—talking all the time about what it was going to mean.

It came time for the supper bell. The first bell rang; they were to put up their tools. But I said, "Wait a minute. Let's all put down our tools now and stand in a ring. And we're all going to say a prayer, and ask God to give us the money for this dormitory as soon as He thinks it's best for us to have it. And also we'll ask Him to teach us to be worthy of a new dormitory, to behave so well that people will want us to have a dormitory. And we'll get the money."

The prayer went around the circle. Not a single boy failed to make his prayer when it came to him. Of course there was lots of repetition, but the prayers were very earnest. As I ended the prayer and looked up, the sun was just setting, a glorious sunset, and the last bell was ringing.

Right then a little boy who had as near nothing in this world as any child could have stepped up and pulled his little fist out of his pants pocket. "Here's you some money to start on," he said. And he handed me a penny.

That penny was our nest egg. It wasn't so very many months later that, coming home from a speaking trip one afternoon and stopping in the car at the office, I heard somebody give a sudden squeal of delight. And rushing out came a stenographer with a check in her hand that she was waving wildly. She brought me the check.

It was for six thousand dollars.

The person who sent the check said it was for a building for our little boys.

It built that building, and it furnished it, and hundreds of little boys have used it since.


## 29

IT was also in the early twenties that we undertook another significant project at Crossnore, one that started very modestly but quickly developed into large proportions.

In 1923, in one of the rooms of our new school building up on the hill, we set up two looms on which we proposed to teach native mountain weaving. That was a natural for our children. Their grandmothers had left many beautiful pieces of weaving, frequently evidencing their makers' great skill,

These pieces had been done after patterns left by the older women, and these patterns in many a mountain home still survived, along with instructions on how to make dyes from things in the woods and from the indigo that they could buy.

But the weaving itself had fallen into disrepute. The old looms were so big and cumbersome, took up so much room in the little homes; and the people wanted more space, sought different things from what they had had in the earlier days. So the old looms had largely been split up for kindling, and the pieces of weaving were preserved only as heirlooms.

Some of our Crossnore girls who were out at Berea College had been taking weaving. By this time, you see, our boys and girls were going off regularly to school and into fields of valuable service. You remember little Hepsy? Well, Hepsy had decided during her schooling at Banner Elk that she wanted to be a trained nurse: I had taken the other children —her younger brothers and sisters—into our school by that time, and she was free to undertake a career. So she went to Dr. Long's hospital in Statesville. A few months after she entered he wrote me a letter. "Mrs. Sloop," he said, "you sent me one little mountain apple that we like very much. Please send us a dozen next time." Other girls did go, and some became trained nurses. And, like Hepsy, most of them got married. But Hepsy, who was to have been a child bride of thirteen, didn't get married until she was old enough to know what she was doing.

But I must get back to our weaving. One of our Crossnore girls at Berea had done particularly well in the weaving course. She seemed just naturally to understand it and love it. So when she finished her schooling there, we decided to start a course at Crossnore; we located two looms and set them up in one of the rooms of our new building.

This girl, Zada Benfield, taught one year. She was a good instructor, and the children worked faithfully and did a surprising amount of good work—in school hours and after.

Zada got married, though, after that first year, and could not continue as instructor. But we were fortunate in getting another who was also good, Mrs. Clara Lowrance from Texas. She taught another year or so, and then she resigned. We were again without an instructor. But here fortune smiled upon Crossnore.

Mrs. Lowrance's most promising pupil had not been a Crossnore student, but one of the women of our community, Mrs. Newbern Johnson. She was wild about weaving. She loved traditional things, the old customs, the old places. The love of native weaving came natural. She had some of the old patterns, and she studied them. I remember once, when we were visiting the North Carolina State Museum in Raleigh, she spent much time studying the old weaving patterns on display there. She was one of the few persons, they told us, who knew enough to be able to "read" those patterns.

She agreed to take over the weaving class. And Aunt Newbie has been in charge ever since. I don't know what we'd have done at Crossnore without her.

Let me make it clear that although I call her "Aunt Newbie," she is much younger than I. The word "Aunt" in the mountains, like "Uncle," is a term of affection and respect. Everybody calls Mrs. Johnson "Aunt Newbie."

She is one of the earth's noble women. Through the long years she has been one of my most faithful and trusted friends and co-workers at Crossnore. Her life is stamped indelibly upon the institution, and on many, many students who have attended it. It is always a delight to me to pay tribute to Aunt Newbie.

She took over the weaving work despite her already very busy schedule as a young wife and mother. Let me tell you what she did in those days. She would get up early in the morning, milk, get breakfast, wash the breakfast dishes, dress the children, take them to her husband's mother's home and leave them there, and then walk a mile and a half to the

173

school, where she would arrive at eight o'clock. All day—until six that night—she would work at those looms. Then she'd go get the children, take them home, feed the stock, milk, help work in the garden (if it was that time of year), cook supper, do her housework, get the children to bed, and then sit down to read in order, as she said, "to improve my education."

Aunt Newbie, I am happy to say, has lived to see all her children turn out exceptionally well in a busy modern world. But she still goes just like she did in the old days; she's busily engaged in teaching weaving and selling the products of our Crossnore looms.

Soon after Aunt Newbie took over, we began to be cramped for space in the school building. We moved the looms into temporary quarters where they stayed about five years, until we had finished our log weaving room. That building, to my mind, was one of the most interesting ever put up in this section of the country. We built it in 1929 out on the highway in order that it would be more easily accessible to the public, for already we were selling Crossnore homespuns, and we meant to sell larger and larger quantities as the course developed. We made it a log house because we felt it would give atmosphere to have our weaving done and displayed in such a building.

It was authentic, too. We got part of the logs from the old McCanless barn. The McCanless house was a famous place in our part of the country. It was where the notorious McCanless gang used to live. The old house is still standing; if it could only tell its story, it would be something worth hearing. But let me leave the weaving a minute and tell you about that house.

I remember first hearing about it years ago. I heard that they were digging up all of the fireplace, and all the rocks around, and were even talking about taking down the chimney. I asked why.

"Everybody that moves into that house," they explained, "always hunts for loot. That's where the McCanless gang used to live."

I said, "The what?"

They said, "The McCanless gang. Didn't you never hear o' them? They was the gang of bank robbers that ran with the James brothers."

I said, "You don't mean Jesse James?"

"Yes, Jesse and Frank and that old Bob Ford." They did hate Bob Ford; they couldn't say enough things against him. He was the one who shot Jesse, "and while he was eatin' his salt," they would say. That's what they said of a person visiting in another's home, "eatin' his salt."

"Well, did the McCanless crowd go with the James boys on their raids?" I asked.

"No," they said, "the James boys used higher up." ("Used" is an expression commonly heard in the mountains to mean *ranged* or, when speaking of cattle, *grazed*.) The Jameses went out from Virginia and across that way, and the McCanless boys went lower down—as low sometimes as Arizona. But then when they came back from a raid, they'd visit each other and tell what they'd done.

"Frank James visited over here a lot durin' his lifetime," they said, "and he come mighty nigh adyin' over here."

I said, "Well, how was that?"

"He'd been over avisitin' the McCanless gang, and he left along about dusky dark on horseback to go home, and by the time he got down on Three Mile Creek it was dark. He knew where Uncle Jacob Carpenter lived, and he climbed into his barn. He realized he was a sick man, but he didn't want to bother the Carpenters. But after a while they come in to feed, and they found him in there. They thought he was agoin' to die. So they took him into Uncle Jake's house and kept him a while, and then he got on his horse and went on home."

After that, they said, Frank James went down into Ala-

175

bama and died there. The James boys were from western Virginia.

"Did you know Jesse James?" I asked one of the men who was telling me about the old house.

"Yes, a little. He come over occasionally. And old Bob Ford come, too. But after Bob shot Jesse James, I bet he'd a better not come around here no more."

"Did you know anything about his shooting Jesse James?" I asked him.

"Yes," he said, "he was avisitin' in Jesse's house, eatin' his salt. And while Jesse James was atryin' to hang a picture in his house, Bob Ford pulled out his pistol and shot him. Jesse James had a pistol in each pocket; he always carried two. But Bob didn't give him no chance, 'cause Jesse's arms was up with the picture when he shot him, and he fell back on the floor afore they could catch him."

That was some of the history of the old McCanless house. And so naturally it was believed that the McCanless gang had hidden a great deal of loot around there. Especially after they had weatherboarded the house over the logs, it was thought they had hidden the loot in the chinks.

So every family that went into the old house would dig up the garden and the hearth and threaten to tear down the chimney, though they haven't done that yet; but they have taken a good many boards off the outside of the house.

It's still here at Crossnore—across the hill over beyond the playground, and a part of the Crossnore property. I some-times wonder if some of that McCanless-gang money isn't buried around that old house somewhere. Maybe one day when I get a little time I'll slip over there myself—with Doctor's shovel—and see if I can't uncover an old iron pot full of gold and silver. . . .

But I've got away from the weaving house. Some of the logs, as I said, came from the old McCanless barn. The rest we got from an old house that had been built for Uncle Will

176

Franklin's grandfather. This house had been used by several newlyweds to begin their housekeeping and had been given to Uncle Will as a home to which to take his bride. Uncle Will helped us move the logs and build the new weaving building from them, and I remember how he protested against cutting the logs in order to put large windows in; he declared to do so would weaken them. Uncle Will had pronounced ideas about building and he did not hesitate to make them known, and emphatically, as he did when he was building our Presbyterian church.

Our weaving classes had been increasing. The girls wanted to learn, then the mothers, and then even several of the boys asked to be allowed to take lessons. Weaving was not only a way to make a little cash, but it was also an interesting avocation, and it was reviving an old custom that they all loved.

We had seen our sales growing, too. People bought everything we made—the old-fashioned counterpanes in the Lee Surrender pattern (coverlets, they called them, or kivvers), homemade blankets, table runners, and curtains. Folks were crazy about them, and they sold well. And now with the new building available for our use, we could have larger classes and increase our output of homespuns.

Six years we used the weaving house. And then in the fall of 1935, while Aunt Newbie and I were attending a big DAR meeting in West Virginia, we got a telegram. Neither of us will ever forget that day. We had left in the weaving building thousands of dollars' worth of finished hand-woven goods, among them twenty-five beautiful coverlets. The telegram said, WEAVING BUILDING BURNED TO GROUND AND EVERYTHING IN IT.

We left almost immediately for home. But the word got out, and those kind DAR ladies took up a collection for Crossnore and gave us three hundred dollars to start our weaving program again.

When we got home, we found that box of coverlets still

smoldering; there wasn't a piece of any size in it that hadn't been burned.

We knew that we were going to build again. And this time we were going to build right on the campus where the people who passed by would have easy access to our products and come in and buy, for we must sell our wares.

We decided we'd build of rock; that wouldn't burn down. But it was October, and the water was cold and the weather was cold. And there was no money for buying stone; we couldn't pay out our precious three hundred dollars for having rock picked up out of the river. The children must do that, and they were eager to.

So when Saturday came of that same week, we had told them, "Now everybody that can be spared, that doesn't have to help get supper, is going right after dinner today down to the river, and we're going to pick up the rocks. I doubt if the little ones ought to go."

But they said they wanted to. They wouldn't be left behind.

And nearly every child did go. There were 120 of them, for Crossnore wasn't so big then as it is now. Those children knew just how to organize themselves in lines that stretched across the river. And into that river they waded, no matter how cold it was. The rocks were picked up on the little island in the middle of the river and passed from hand to hand until they were put up on the bank. Then a truck came and picked them up and hauled them away.

Truckloads of varying sizes of rocks were piled into a mound. We begged the children to quit and go home because it was getting so cold. But they wouldn't leave as long as they could see how to handle the rocks. And not a child took a cold. We were very careful of them when they came back; gave them hot baths and had them rub each other down. And nobody got sick.

Now we could spend that three hundred dollars on cement. We did, and began to build. But they were afraid the cement would freeze; we kept fires around it at night, besides covering it up, and in the daytime we got to making cement with boiling water.

So we kept on until we had a weaving building. And we have it today.

Not only children and young people learned to weave, but old people came who could remember that their grandmothers did it. One old lady with a big family had two children working in the weaving room after school hours in the afternoon, and then they'd trudge home over the hill in time to help with the evening milking. This old lady decided she wanted to learn. She said they'd have to bring the loom to her house because she couldn't leave the little childen. There was no road to her house, but the children carried the parts of that loom, and Aunt Newbie went over and helped put it together again. The old lady took her lessons. She began weaving.

We didn't hear much about what was going on up there until one of her girls came with her arms full of Lee Surrender rugs, for that was what the old lady was to make. They were well made, too, and she got a check for them. Every now and then another armful came, and she made only Lee Surrender rugs. But they sold, and the check would go back. And then one day the other child, a bright-eyed little girl who looked much too young to weave, came to see Aunt Newbie. And she said, "Aunt Newbie, I want you to take a good look at these rugs and see which one you think is made the best, which one is beat the hardest." For beating—pushing the threads together—would add to the life of the rug.

Aunt Newbie looked them through, picked out one, said, "I think this is the best one."

"Goody," the little girl said. "That's the one I made; I told 'em it was the best."

Looking at that child's thin arms, you'd never have thought

179

she could do the beating necessary for such a rug. Then Aunt Newbie said, "Why, you're too little to weave."

"No," she said, "I'm not. We keep that loom agoin' all the time. Soon's one quits the other begins. And we weave."

Aunt Newbie said, "Would you like to have your check for this rug separate from your mother's check?"

"No," she said. "Put them all together. The last check finished payin' for the floorin'. This check's agoin' to start the windows."

Their house was finished before the old one fell down, as we all feared it would in a short while. And many homes have been built with weaving money since that one.

Weaving has become an important source of revenue, under the skillful management of Aunt Newbie. But more important, I think, is the fact that it has revived in our mountain country one of the great old customs of the region. Here within less than a hundred miles of the great modern textile-manufacturing center of the south, we are producing on cumbersome old hand looms beautiful and authentic homespuns eagerly sought after by countless visitors to our campus.

We are right proud of the things we are making with our hands at Crossnore.

## 30

AS I sit here in my office in the Administration Building and recall the significant happenings of those days when we were establishing the foundations of Crossnore, I keep returning to that period of the twenties. Perhaps that was our most important decade. Certainly it saw for us many great things dreamed and initiated. Nor was it without its vexing problems.

One of the things that troubled us, particularly as physicians in a pioneer country, was our lack of any suitable place in which to take care of sick people, whether it was those on the campus or those who for miles around needed our care.

We were having marvelous success in our medical work. Despite no adequate facilities for treating the sick, for caring for them after operations, or for getting them in shape to undergo surgery, despite lack of sanitation in their homes that endangered not only those ill but all the others around them, despite what must have been billions of all kinds of germs contaminating their mountain homes, they generally got well. Doctor and I marveled that some recovered. We were confident that Providence had a stronger hand in effecting cures than we had.

So we hoped and prayed and figured and schemed how we could establish a little hospital in the community. And one day while we were thus engaged, we received a letter. Opening it, we discovered a check for five thousand dollars. "This is money left me by my parents," the lady wrote. "I want you to use it toward building a hospital for Crossnore—not just one for the school but one for all the people in the country around."

She was a city lady, and little did she know what it would cost to build a hospital. But the five thousand dollars gave us a start, and we were most thankful for it. The hospital was begun.

In 1928 we opened that hospital. If I could look straight through the walls in front of me, I could see that little hospital right now; and if my eyesight could penetrate its walls, I very likely this moment would see my two children, both of them doctors, busily at work there. In all probability Emma, who is in charge during the daytime, is treating someone in her office or visiting a patient in one of the rooms or wards. And Will, I suspect, is drilling away on some poor fellow's tooth. Ugh-h-h! The very thought of that drill buzzing merrily along one-sixteenth of an inch away from a highly sensitive nerve is already giving me the fidgets!

When five o'clock comes, Emma will take off her white coat and go down the hill to Dwight and the youngsters, and Doctor will take her place—until she returns tomorrow morning. That is the routine. (I know there are a lot of doctors in this world, four in my family, in fact, but my husband shall always remain Doctor.)

Our hospital has offices for three doctors and a dentist, an X-ray room and laboratory, eight private rooms and two wards, and is equipped adequately for twenty beds, not counting the bassinets. From the beginning the people have flocked to it. And they have been so grateful for its services.

I recall two occasions soon after the hospital was opened when it was especially crowded. One was when there were nineteen new babies there. As I said, it was a twenty-bed hospital, and we had ten bassinets—homemade bassinets. The ten filled, and still other babies came. A pair of twins one night, and the next night another pair of twins, and a day or two after that—yes, it's the truth—a set of triplets. We took a bed into one of the rooms and put the babies crosswise on it so that it looked like a banana wagon.

Everybody was at work; everybody was trying to wait on the mothers and take care of those precious babies. The staff of the hospital then consisted of Dr. Sloop and me. We had one nurse and some girls who worked there, and we certainly put in the time day and night. But the babies all went out healthy—healthier than their doctors, I do believe.

But that other crowded time came. The mumps broke out in the school. All the campus children seemed susceptible. We couldn't keep them in the dormitories, because it would spread worse than ever. So we began sending them to the hospital. Then the nurse sent word that she had twenty-nine cases of mumps, that they were all over the halls and everywhere else. Please, she said, don't send any more.

That caused us to realize more than ever that we needed a school infirmary. Patients came and asked to be admitted to the hospital, and we wanted to take them in. But what could we do? Every bed was full of mumps, and some beds had two cases in them. There were even two cases on our rolling stretchers.

The lesson we learned from that was that we must not be satisfied with just the hospital. The neighbors for many miles around needed our attention—hospital attention—and the school children must not be allowed to crowd them out.

So we decided that we just must have an infirmary. But, as usual, there was no money in sight. Things were at a pretty low ebb. We couldn't even afford a pastor then in our new Presbyterian church Uncle Will Franklin had just built. Members of our faculty were taking turns holding service. The text Mr. Bault chose on his Sunday—he's now a professor down at the University of Florida—was "Except the Lord build the house they labor in vain that build it."

That verse kept ringing in my ears. I couldn't dismiss it from my mind. So I kept the talk going about the idea of an infirmary, and after several consultations we decided we'd go ahead and build it.

There had to be some excavating done, I knew, but we wouldn't have to buy anything for that. The boys could do that work. We had a carpentry class that was perfectly willing to undertake the building of an infirmary as their project for the year. But who was going to provide the material?

"The Lord will provide it," I said.

So when supper was over one evening, I said, "We're all going up on the grounds near the playground. We're going to start the excavation now for the infirmary. But before we start, we're going to dedicate the land."

We went, everybody. Even the dishwashing was postponed. We gathered around some trees there on the lot where it was to be built. Every boy lined up, big and little. All the shovels, all the picks and mattocks, had been collected, and the boys were standing there with these tools in their hands.

Then we had our little service. I read the verse that had been in my mind constantly since Mr. Bault had made his discourse from it. We all learned to say it; we repeated it until everybody knew it. Then Aunt Newbie offered a prayer.

I'll never forget that little service. We were to earn our part by our service to God, by dedicating our hearts and our lives to God. Even the smallest children were impressed.

Then we began our work. We were going to do our part just as far as we could. And we did it. The boys manfully dug into that earth and turned it over. Other boys came up and took the shovels and dug, until the ditch on the outside that had been marked off by strings had been started the full length. When this was done, we sang the good old gospel hymns, and went back to our work, including washing dishes.

The boys of the carpentry class came up there the next morning. They took those same tools. They dug as long as they could handle the rocky earth, which became more rocky as they excavated. Finally we had to let them quit, and the big, strong men dug the rest of those ditches.

But we got it all done—and it hadn't taken too long. Next we had to dig a furnace room. That took the strongest kind of digging. We had to dig out an entrance, for there was a hump where there ought to have been a hollow. It seemed as if we would never be through with the digging . . . and after that, what of the money?

One day we opened the mail, and a check for a thousand dollars dropped out. The note with it said, "This is for the infirmary." The next week another one came. And from then on, almost once a week until six had come, we got a thousand-dollar check, each one marked "For the infirmary."

Now we knew that the infirmary was going to be built. The checks had come from different people and different parts of the country.

Those thousand-dollar checks impressed us so. It was tremendous—a thousand dollars! And six of them! To get six thousand dollars in six checks not more than a week or so apart made us remember that we had asked God to send us the money and He had done His part.

The boys did their part, too, and they kept on through the summer, and in the fall we had an infirmary that could take care of twenty-nine cases of mumps—or anything else that might come along. Fortunately mumps paid only one visit. . . .

Raising money is never a matter of simply opening letters and having checks fall out, as I may have indicated in telling of several incidents, dramatic to us, in which that happened. I am confident that those checks, and many others through the years, came as answers to our prayers—and our work, because we worked to get them!

Sometimes I wonder how many letters I have written asking for help for Crossnore and how many others I have written thanking friends of Crossnore for their contributions to our work. Raising money is not a falling-off-a-log job. It requires letter writing, speechmaking, travel, and—above all—faith in your cause. We were always long on that last item at Crossnore.

Maybe you'd be interested in our daily routine at Crossnore in those early years. We live busy lives nowadays, but they are almost slow and idle compared to what we used to do. Why don't I just describe an average morning—to give you the idea?

We got up early. School started at eight o'clock, and I had to have the children there by that time. Our house was about a mile from the school, and usually they walked. Often, especially when they were small, I went with them.

But I had been up and stirring a long time before the hour for leaving for school. I tried not to awaken Doctor, who often had calls late in the night and in the early-morning hours and greatly needed all the sleep he could get. There was breakfast to prepare for the children, and while we kept four of the teachers at our home (because they had no other place to live), there was breakfast to be cooked for them and lunch boxes to be filled.

So I had to get up at four o'clock to get after the routine chores. One thing that bothered me, I remember, was the old stovepipe. It seemed to me that I had to clean out that pipe almost every morning before I could start cooking breakfast. I wasn't any too good at cooking, either; we often had batter bread and waffles and other things that took a long time to cook and serve; I didn't know how to simplify my breakfast routine.

But the biggest bother was the people coming early for Doctor. Frequently they would come by the time I had got up, and they would insist on seeing Doctor. I remember that one morning one of our elder citizens came to the house at five o'clock and declared he just had to see Doctor. I told him that Doctor had been out late the night before and needed his sleep. I refused to awaken him. The old man grumbled. "Mis' Sloops," he said, "if Dr. Sloop don't learn to get up like us folk around here, he won't do no good in this country." But I stood firm, and the old fellow had to wait around until Doctor was ready to get up.

After I had either walked the children to school or got them off under their own steam, I did the breakfast dishes and cleaned the house. If it was washday—and it seemed that washdays came mighty often—I did the washing and hung out the clothes to dry.

Then I sat down to write letters. I wrote friends at Davidson, friends in Charlotte, countless friends and acquaintances everywhere; I asked them for money, I asked for old clothes, I asked them to establish small scholarships to aid pupils, especially certain boys and girls getting ready to go off to college. I wrote various DAR ladies and DAR chapters. All the time I was writing letters asking for things, I was writing other letters thanking friends for contributions and telling them how their gifts were bringing results in our mountain section.

Frequently my letter writing was interrupted by patients. Sometimes it would be an emergency, like treating a man who had injured a hand or foot while at work or hunting, some injury not serious enough to require Doctor's surgery; sometimes it would be prescribing medicine. My letter writing would be interrupted too when Doctor got up and had to be fed. He customarily ate only two meals a day, or rather two meals in twenty-four hours, because frequently one of these meals would be in the middle of the night.

I remember that one of my greatest trials was trying to learn how to wash and iron. I got a neighbor to give me lessons, but I'll confess I was never good at it, nor did I ever learn to like it. But it was one of those things, nevertheless, that had to be done, and so I did it—after a fashion. I did much of our sewing too. I made all Doctor's shirts, except those that now and then he was able to buy out of the old-clothes sale at Aunt Pop's and Uncle Gilmer's store. And I made my dresses, though frequently I could fit myself in dresses and suits down at the old-clothes store, too.

Having got Doctor fed and off to his duties, I would treat what patients there remained with minor complaints, and then I would turn my back on medicine and household affairs and plunge into my work at the school. By noontime . . . but why go on? I'm just making myself tired thinking about it. We were busy, let's leave it at that.

# 31

ONE of the greatest hindrances to our work has always been our very limited funds. Certainly that is not in any sense peculiar to Crossnore either as an institution or as a community. It has applied to Doctor and me personally, though we have always managed to get along. And we have, thanks to Providence and a multitude of wonderful friends, had a good life.

At Crossnore we have had to figure and fight for every advance. That has given zest to our living. But sometimes we would have been tempted to accept a little more of security and a little less of zest.

The same thing has been true of our mountain region, especially back two or three decades ago. Many of our people were very poor, as I have pointed out, because of bad roads and inadequate marketing facilities, and though I have always fought moonshining and am in no mind to justify it now, I should make it clear that it was so much easier to make corn into whisky and sell it to people who would come up here for it than to attempt to haul the corn itself off to market.

The temptation was great, and many persons, many of them otherwise excellent citizens, took part in the making of whisky.

My stand—well known through the mountains—was encouraging to the brave men and women who had always opposed whisky making and would endure the direst poverty and privations rather than make liquor and take money for it. They were always risking maltreatment and were constantly in danger because of their efforts to stop whisky making. They made efforts too—determined efforts—to stop it, but they didn't often succeed. They needed help, and I tried to give it.

In the early days one old lady said to me once, "You have to be bothered at night just like I've always been."

I said, "What bothers you at night?"

"Why, they're al'ays acomin' for your husband at night to wait on some sick one or to fetch a young 'un, or somethin'," she said. "And that's the way it is with my ol' man, though"

188

—she grinned—"it's for a different reason. They're al'ays acomin' for him at night, too."

"Why are they coming for him at night?" I asked her. I knew her husband was not a doctor.

"Well," she replied, "my ol' man is noted over this whole country for abein' the hones'est man anywheres. So when they finished a run of liquor, they'd al'ays pretty generally send for him. A lot of times they'd have trouble adividin' it, and they'd get to fightin' over it, and real often somebody got killed. So that's why they got in a habit of sendin' for Isaac to come and divide the run. They knowed he wouldn't tell on 'em. He'd lecture 'em 'bout makin' it, 'bout it bein' the wrong thing to do. He'd do all he could to persuade 'em to make an honest livin', but still he'd go and divide that run and come away from a peaceable time. He told me that he b'lieved he'd prevented many a murder in this country and he did hope the Lord'd give him credit for it."

Old Isaac performed a unique service, but a service it was!

Among those who made their living wholly by making liquor were some very interesting characters, some with good brains and capable of doing many worth-while things in this world if they'd only had a fair chance.

I remember on one occasion I was sent for to come to the county jail. It was during a term of court, and I was in the courthouse. I had gone there, as I often did, to help prosecute moonshiners.

This young boy—from Canada, he claimed to be—wanted me to help him get sent back there. While I was talking with him, the prisoners gathered in that one cage until it was full. Standing at the back, looking out over the heads of them all, was a tall, straight man who looked like the picture of a Roman soldier.

"Mis' Sloop," he said, "if you don't mind, may I ask you a question?"

"Certainly you may," I said.

"Don't you think I'm abein' persecuted rather than prosecuted at this term of court?"

"No, I don't," I said. "Why do you think so?"

" 'Cause," he said, "that warrant says that I made liquor in Avery County." And raising his hand above his head, he said, "And 'fore God I can testify that I never made a drop of liquor in Avery County in my life."

"Well," I said, "Mr. Clark" (I am calling him Jeb Clark here, though that wasn't his name), "since you brought God into the case, I don't think it makes any difference to Him whether you made liquor in Avery County or in Mitchell County. You used the brain that God gave you—which is far better than many men have—to degrade yourself, to degrade the boys whom you taught to make liquor, and to make yourself an evil influence in this country when you might have been a power for good."

"Well," he said, "maybe you're right. Maybe I oughtn't to do it." Real pious talk for him. "But if you'll tell the judge not to give me more than a one-year sentence"—he might have said two, I'm vague on it—"I promise you I'll serve that sentence."

"You don't have to serve that sentence," I said. "You don't have to serve any sentence. You know how to get out of any jail or prison that's built in North Carolina, and you know you do. You've already gotten out of a good many. If you'll serve your term and pay your debt to the state, though, you'll be a more self-respecting citizen."

"Well," he says, "if he don't give me over a year, I promise you I'll serve every day of it."

"I don't believe I could have any influence with the judge," I said, "but I'll try, and we'll see what'll happen."

What I said to the judge must have had little or no effect upon him. At any rate, he gave Jeb two years.

I wrote a letter to the warden of the penitentiary in Raleigh—because Jeb was an old-timer—and told the warden that Jeb would get away from him as sure as anything in this world, and to keep him, so as to teach him a lesson and give the boys in the country a better chance to grow up without being taught how to make liquor.

At Christmastime I got a letter from Jeb, written in red ink, telling me that he was now out at Caledonia Prison Farm and that he was looking forward to a happy Christmas. But, he said, he would love to spend it at home. He wanted me to promise to take his son into the school here. He wrote, "I'd like to have a boy that's made a better record than I have, and I want you to train him."

I investigated and found that his son was then in jail awaiting trial for doing the same thing his daddy had been doing. I didn't take the boy into the school, and I didn't make any effort to. But I did warn the prison warden about letting Jeb get out around Christmastime, that that was the time he was apt to decide to come home. They were sending men up into this country from the prison to work the mica mines, and Jeb, I found out later, said to the warden, "What makes you send those men up there that come here from cities and towns and down the country and don't know anything at all about mining? Why don't you send mountain men up there to work in the mines, and you'd get a day's work that was worth something to you?"

So the poor innocent warden sent Jeb to the mines in Mitchell County.

He worked well for two weeks—made a brilliant record as to the amount of mica he mined. At the end of that two weeks he picked up his dinner bucket and said, "Well, fellows, I'm agoin', and you won't see me no more."

And he went.

I didn't stop until we got hold of him again and sent him back to finish that term. But it wasn't long before they caught him making liquor again and sent him once more to the peni-

191

tentiary. This time he got out on the score that his mother had died of pneumonia and he wanted to go to the funeral. Within less than a month after the mother died, the father also died of pneumonia. So Jeb stayed to that funeral, and by that time it was so near to the day for his term to be out that they just didn't bother to take him back.

Some time after Jeb's release, I was being driven down to Crossnore to work one day when this man waved me down. I stopped, and he came up. I didn't recognize him. I hadn't seen him in a long time. He chatted with me a little while. Then he said, "I don't believe you know who I am."

"No," I said, "I don't believe I do. I know your face, but I can't fit your name to it."

He turned to the man who was driving me and said, "If I'd sent a fellow to the penitentiary as often as she's sent me, I do believe I'd remember his name." At least Jeb did have a sense of humor.

Another time when this fellow was sent down to the Raleigh jail he escaped once more and then disappeared from this part of the country. But one morning a man came to my office and brought me a piece of paper. "I picked this up in my cornfield this morning," he said.

DEAR LADY.

I hate to be passing so near to your house and not come in to pay my respecks. But I'm in a hurry to get to Tennessee so I thought I'd just leave you a note. I'll leave it here in Jim's cornfield and he'll be apt to pick it up when he comes out to hoe. I hope he will take it to you. With my highest regards.

JEB

He must have stayed in Tennessee some little time. We were coming back from Johnson City one afternoon, and somebody waved at us. But we were in our little, Model-T Ford, so this big husk of a man couldn't possibly have sat with us. We didn't stop for him. But as we passed him by, I recog-

192

nized my friend, recently escaped from Raleigh. I investigated and found out that he was then serving as a policeman in Johnson City.

I knew he'd be a very successful one, for he certainly knew all the ins and outs—especially the outs.

## 32

JEB CLARK was only one of many mountain characters who lived in and around Crossnore. They have helped make living in the mountains to me so rewarding. The people are so interesting—so real and genuine, so always themselves.

I suppose I could go on for hours naming unique characters and describing them. And it would be for me a pleasant chore. Many of them I've already introduced. But they're only a small part of those I could talk about. Uncle John Carroll, for instance, was one of the old citizens who used to help us look up the graves of Revolutionary soldiers. He had a wooden leg and walked with two canes, but he almost invariably ran the legs off those young women who went grave-hunting with him. He would take them over fences, over rock walls, across fields and ditches, through thickets and brambles and over streams, until he'd have them fairly gasping for breath. And when they'd protest that *he* must be tired and wouldn't *he* like to stop a few minutes, he'd say, "Law, Honey, I don't need to rest none. When my meat leg gits tired, I just stands on my wooden one."

And Aunt Sarah Jones. She was a loud-talking, snuff-dipping old lady who simply never felt well, she said, but was as inexhaustible as Uncle John Carroll. She could do more hard work than half the men in the county, and yet she was always complaining of being "po'ly."

There were countless others. But among them all, one of my especial favorites was Uncle Newt Clark, the man who was so anxious to have Latin taught at Crossnore. He was no relation to Jeb the moonshiner; Jeb Clark wasn't the fellow's name anyway, as I explained; I just used that name to give him a handle.

Uncle Newt was perhaps our best-informed local historian. He was just a natural gatherer of historical facts and was so anxious to remember them that he had his daughter Flora keep a book and write in it all the things that he heard about how the folks did in olden times.

Flora was educated; she'd been to high school. But Uncle Newt couldn't read or write.

One afternoon he came home and said to his wife, Mary Jane, "Git me some money. I want to go up to Aunt 'Nerv's and buy her clock. I hear she's agoin' to die tonight, and I must git there 'fore she does and have her tell all them folks that's gathered around that she wants me to have that clock."

The clock in question was one which Sandy Clark had brought over with him from England during the Revolutionary War, and all the relatives, Uncle Newt knew, would like to have it. It was entirely a wooden clock. All the wheels and everything else about it were of wood. Aunt 'Nerv' had inherited it from her father, who had gotten it from Uncle Sandy, and Aunt 'Nerv' didn't aim to let anybody else have it.

So now she was about to die at a ripe old age—it was very ripe—and Uncle Newt thought the time had come for him to go and get the clock. He got the four one-dollar bills that Aunt Mary Jane found for him, and started out. He said he walked 17 miles.

When he got to Aunt 'Nerv's house, the people were crowding around the bed of the old lady who was supposed to be breathing her last. So Uncle Newt pushed them to one side and said, "Let me git in here. I've got to talk to Aunt 'Nerv'. She's agoin' to die, they tell me, and I want her to tell you 'nes that that clock b'longs to me—'cause she's promised it to me."

As he approached Aunt 'Nerv's bed, he found her in very serious condition. He leaned down over her and called in a loud voice, "Aunt 'Nerv'! Aunt 'Nerv'! This is Newt. You know you promised me that clock when you died. And they say you're agoin' to die tonight. I want you to tell all the folks around here that's my clock, and I'm agoin' to have it and take it away with me."

She didn't say a word.

So he pulled out the money that Mary Jane had given him and tried a new tack. "Aunt 'Nerv'! Aunt 'Nerv'!" he said into her ear. "Wake up, Aunt 'Nerv'! I've got something I got to tell you. Now, you listen. I brung you four dollars, and here's the money." And he took her hand and put the greenbacks in it and folded it over. She tried to put it under the pillow, which was her favorite place for keeping money, but her hand wouldn't go. So he helped her push it up under the pillow.

And the hand was never brought down.

Then he said to her again: "Wake up, Aunt 'Nerv'. I done paid you for that clock. Now, tell these folks that the clock is mine, that you promised it to Newt and you're agoin' to leave it to Newt."

After a moment's silence, with some effort she said, "The clock's Newt's."

And then she died.

Some years later Uncle John Wise was reported to be desperately ill, and they said he couldn't live through the night. And again Uncle Newt took interest, and when he came home, he said, "Flora, get the book. We're agoin' down to Uncle John Wise's tonight. You know we've got a whole lot in this book that Uncle John told us, but there's some questions I want to aks him, and I can't do it if I don't go tonight."

Flora and Mary Jane wanted to know why.

" 'Cause," he said, "they say he's agoin' to die tonight, and I want to git them questions answered 'fore he dies."

So Flora got her book, and he got his lantern.

When they got down to Uncle John's, he took out his knife, stuck the blade into the wall, and hung the lantern on it. Then he walked up to Uncle John's bed—and again the neighbors were all gathered around, watching the old man draw apparently his last breath.

"Get out of the way!" he said. "I've got some questions I want to aks Uncle John."

They said, "Why, Uncle John's adyin'!"

"I don't care," he said. "He might tell me somethin' 'fore he dies."

So Uncle John, being very deaf, had to be yelled to very loudly. But Newt made Uncle John hear him as he said, "Uncle John, wake up! I got some questions to aks you, and they tell me you're agoin' to die tonight. So I want you to answer 'em now."

Then Uncle John said, "All right, Newt, aks 'em."

So Newt began to ask Uncle John questions—about this one and that one, and who married whom, and so forth. And Uncle John answered every question, very slowly and with a good deal of difficulty because of shortness of breath. But he answered them.

Away along in the middle of the night he got awful thirsty, and he called for water. In those days they didn't believe in giving dying people water. But, as Uncle Newt said afterward, he didn't see how it could do any harm if they were dying. So he decided to give Uncle John a cup of water.

But there was no water in the cabin. And nobody dared leave the old man for fear he would die in the meantime. The only thing Uncle Newt could find was about a quart of sweet cider vinegar. So he poured some into a cup, held up the old man's head, and put the cup to his lips. Uncle John sipped it weakly. "Tastes mighty good," he said. "Git me a little more."

196

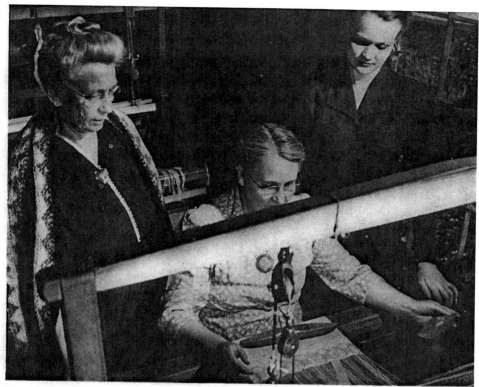

Dr. Sloop (*left*) watches some old-fashioned hand weaving which
is taught at Crossnore (*above*). A field of Sequoyah Irish potatoes
at Crossnore, in part the result of Dr. Sloop's tireless campaigns
for modern farming methods and better roads (*below*).

The two Doctors Sloop photographed in a restaurant in Asheville the night she received the news of the American Mother of the Year Award.

So Uncle Newt poured more into the cup, and all in all Uncle John must have drunk almost the whole quart.

Throughout the night he got better and better, and toward daylight he called for his breakfast. "I'm hungry," he announced. "Git me somethin' t'eat."

Then he got out of bed, ate his breakfast—and lived seven years longer. . . .

But the characters weren't all old people. There was Ladybird, for instance. The folks in these parts will be a long time forgetting Ladybird. I'm certain I never shall forget her.

She was just a little spindly girl in her early teens. She wasn't pretty, though she was presentable enough when she was fixed up, but she had a lot of fire, and she certainly wasn't lacking in imagination. As a child, Ladybird (I don't believe I ever knew what her real name was) had few opportunities. So she left her home and went to live with Uncle Robert Wiseman and his wife, Aunt Lottie. If ever a couple was beloved in all the country round about, it was Uncle Robert and Aunt Lottie.

And with their usual desire to do good in the world, they took Ladybird in and decided they would teach her to do housework. That was terribly hard on Ladybird; she never wanted to be still a minute. But if they'd let her do the roughest chores around, she'd work.

Finally Aunt Lottie sent her up here to Crossnore to school. But Ladybird couldn't stand that at all. She stayed through one Sunday, and then Ladybird flew. She told someone that "they didn't do nothin' in that place but wash dishes" and she "wa'n't born to wash dishes." So she wouldn't stay.

One day at Uncle Robert's she was listening, I suppose, to some of the legendary stories, some of the traditions about the old people. They would talk constantly of William Wiseman, the great-grandfather of Uncle Robert, who was buried in the yard of Uncle Robert's home. Uncle William was the patriarch of that family, and the stories about him were numerous. One of them was that he had had a very valuable watch, among other things, and this watch had been buried with him.

Ladybird decided that she wanted that watch. She told some of her friends, and another girl also got imbued with the idea that they ought to see that wonderful watch.

So one night—nobody knows at what hour—the two girls went out in the yard and opened the grave and dug up the remains of old Uncle William, who had been buried more than a hundred years.

There were one or two bones left in such a shape that you could recognize them, and particularly one long thighbone. They couldn't find anything that resembled a watch, though, and it made Ladybird awful mad. She allowed she wasn't going to do all that digging for nothing.

"I'm agoin' to have somethin' out of here anyhow," she told the other girl, "and this'll make an awful good baseball bat."

So she took the thighbone out, and they filled up the grave. And when Uncle Robert and Aunt Lottie next saw Ladybird, she was actually playing baseball with Uncle William's thighbone.

Of course, it was promptly returned to its grave, and Ladybird was sent apacking. But she had had her fun, and she had made for herself a spot in Crossnore history. . . .

Now I must tell briefly the story of one of the sweetest characters I've ever known. His memory is a blessing and a benediction.

His name was Roadman, and he came to us when he was about seven. From the day he came, he walked straight into our hearts. He was a tiny youngster, and we saw at once that he was frail and would require much attention. An examination revealed that his tonsils would have to come out, and so we sent him to the little hospital.

As he lay there on those white sheets—the child had never seen such a white bed, I'm sure—the nurse came to him to procure his history. Her notebook in hand, she stood above him.

"What's your name, little man?"

"Roadman, ma'am—Roadman Hollander," he replied.

"Roadman? You mean Rodman, don't you, sonny?"

"No'm, Roadman. My mammy was up on the mountain apickin' huckleberries, and she got sick sudden-like and started for home, but she couldn't quite get to the barn. So she just laid down and had me on the road, and when my daddy come he laughed and named me Roadman, and I'se been Roadman ever since."

Never has there been a child on the campus at Crossnore who so won the hearts of everybody. He was a completely sweet boy, with charming natural manners and grace. And he was smart. He had a brilliant mind. His teachers quickly marked him as an unusual child. He was the sort who was always asking questions—sensible questions that got to the heart of a situation. Whenever we had distinguished visitors on the campus, you'd invariably find little Roadman there. Pretty soon he would have squeezed unobtrusively into the center of things and begun to ask questions. When they went away, he knew much more than when they had come. Three of his teachers unequivocally predicted that Roadman would be President of the United States.

But that was not to be.

When he was twelve, appendicitis overtook him. He went back to the hospital, and once more we prepared him for an operation. Once more he spelled out his name proudly to the lady in the white uniform—"R-o-a-d-m-a-n."

But he didn't get to have that operation. He went down fast, rallied, and then began to lose ground. Two older boys were staying in the room with him, and they noticed that the nurse came in and out often and soon Doctor came in. When

Doctor went out, little Roadman, the boys reported, seemed to exert all the strength he had left and spoke to them. "I know I'm agoin' to die tonight," he said, "but I'm not afraid and I'm not agoin' to be yellow."

So he left us.

We had a little funeral service, and the big tears filled the eyes of the children. But they made not a sound. Then we carried him away to his mountain home in an isolated section of our county and laid him to rest on the top of a lonely peak beside the mother who had died before he came to Crossnore.

"We will never forget Roadman," I told the sorrowing children. "Someday we'll have money enough to build a good dormitory that will be a home for the Middle Boys, and we'll name it Roadman Home." Roadman's father heard about the idea and brought me ten dollars. That was our first gift. Each year we hoped we could get going on it, but for a number of years we failed. That ten dollars didn't go very far, but it was a beginning. We felt that we had a sacred trust. So after a while we started work—dug the excavations, poured the foundations. Sometimes we'd have to stop because there was no money. I remember writing a letter that we sent out to friends of Crossnore some years ago. In it I told of having had to stop work on the building because we couldn't pay the money. And then, a few days later, I received a large contribution from a young businessman who was interested in our work. I called the workmen back to their jobs.

Roadman's sisters, too, were so hopeful that we might be able to build the structure in memory of their little brother. Two of them were in school at Crossnore when he died. They have graduated and become successful nurses. One is head nurse of the operating room at the Banner Elk Hospital.

We have all had our wishes fulfilled. The Middle Boys have a handsome and comfortable dormitory.

Every time I go by Roadman Home, I think of that sweet child and what he has meant to us and what he might have become with his exceptional mind. And I pause again in reverent wonderment to ponder anew the inscrutable mystery of death —and life.

# 33

BUT no one generation or period in the long history of the settlements in the mountains has had a monopoly on "characters." We have had them since the earliest days. I think we have proof of that statement in the numerous ballads that have come down to us.

The people of the Southern Appalachians have been justly praised for their great love of the old ballads. It is largely because of their faithfulness to the tradition of handing them down to their children and their children's children that many of these quaint stories in song have survived. Everybody, of course, has heard of the sore trials and tribulations of Frankie Silvers before, during, and after she "done in" Johnny, her man who "done her wrong." "Frankie and Johnny" is one of the best-known American ballads.

Well, Frankie Silvers, though we have no pride in saying so, was a North Carolina mountain girl who has the unenviable record of having been the first woman to be hanged in North Carolina. She is buried, tradition has it, not far from the Blue Ridge Parkway and in the vicinity of Crossnore.

Many of the older people in our country continue to sing the various versions of the story of Frankie's murder of her husband, and record players and juke boxes throughout the land loudly recite the harrowing details. Some of our mountain people declare that Frankie herself composed the poem and recited it on the scaffold a few moments before she plunged to her death. Perhaps the exact facts will never be known, and in that respect the famous ballad of "Frankie and Johnny" is a perfect example of the old English ballad, a story in song based upon fact but colored and changed through the years as it is handed down from one generation to another.

About a century and a quarter ago—the murder is said to have occurred in December, 1831—Frankie and her husband started housekeeping in a cabin on the 'Toe River not many miles from our first mountain home at Plumtree. Strange to say, her husband's name was not Johnny, but Charlie. They were very happy. Charlie was a handsome fellow, the various versions agree, although few of them describe him in the same way. Frankie was "counted very pretty."

But Charlie was popular with the women. At mountain gatherings he played his "guit-tar," and sang and danced to the delight particularly of the fair sex. Frankie began to get jealous. And when Charlie got to staying away from home longer than Frankie thought warranted and when he was unable satisfactorily to explain where he had been and why, she became furious.

Some accounts say that Charlie had returned from one of these mysterious trips and had fallen asleep in front of the open fire. Others say he had been cutting wood all day and they had quarreled, and then he had lain down in front of the fire. Anyway, they agree that he was asleep in front of the fire when Frankie decided to even things with her "Johnny who'd done her wrong."

She didn't use that pistol (that went "root-ta-toot-toot"), but she got the ax in the corner and swung it at the sleeping man with all her might. She meant to cut off his head with one blow, but she hit him a glancing blow. The mortally wounded man got to his feet and stumbled about the room until the whole place was bloody, and then he fell across the bed and died.

Frankie was in a panic. What would she do? How could she explain? What would she tell Charlie's folks, her folks, the sheriff?

She sat a long time, and thought. Then she arose, went over to the bed, pulled the dead man's body out into the middle of the floor, and went to work—with the ax. All night she chopped up Charlie and threw the dismembered sections into the blazing fire. And then she began to wash away the blood —from the bedclothes, the walls, the puncheon floor.

The next morning, having finished her gruesome task, she went to her father-in-law's house and reported that the night before Charlie had crossed the 'Toe River on the ice to go to visit a neighbor. He hadn't returned, she said, and she was worried.

They started a search, but Charlie wasn't to be found. Frankie mourned, and as the days passed she mourned loudly —too loudly, some of the people began to suspect. Charlie's father and other relatives decided to search the cabin. They soon began to discover things. The mantelboard had been scrubbed, and there were even places where the wood had been whittled off. Places on the walls showed knife or ax marks. The cabin floor had recently been scoured, and when somebody thought of pulling up one of the puncheons, they discovered drying blood on the rounded undersides. They put out the fire and began to examine the ashes. Teeth and pieces of bone were soon discovered.

They called the sheriff. Frankie screamed and shouted her denials, but the sheriff carried her to Morganton and locked her in the jail. In June, 1832, the trial came off. Frankie was convicted, and the judge sentenced her to be hanged. But tradition has it that before the sentence could be carried out, Frankie escaped, with the aid of conniving relatives. Soon, however, she was recaptured, and this time she knew she would never break jail again. She became calm, even indifferent to her fate. One day she called for a pencil and paper. She was going to write a poem, she said.

When they came for her to take her to the scaffold, she had the paper in her hand. She was also carrying a piece of cake, left from her last meal. She mounted the thirteen steps boldly, walked erect to the place where the noose was hanging ready. The sheriff asked her if there was anything he could do for her as a last act. Yes, she said, he could let her finish eating her cake, which was mighty good, and let her read her poem.

He said she might. So in calm, clear voice she read "Frankie and Johnny." Then she finished the last bite of cake, snatched the black hood from the sheriff's trembling hand, jerked it down over her head. An instant later and her body plunged through the trap.

That's the story. And, they say up here in the mountains, it is very near to the facts, though various versions of "Frankie and Johnny," notably those that have the poor couple living in a city and the girl accomplishing her husband's demise after hurrying home "to get ahold of Johnny's shooting gun," depart quite a way from the true 'Toe River locale of the tragedy.

But not all mountain ballads are tragic in theme and tone. One of the more famous, for instance, tells in verse after verse —and that is a characteristic of these ballads, that they go on and on—of the sterling, if somewhat unpolished, character of a mountain patriarch known only as Great-granddad. It used to be sung without accompaniment, or to the strumming of a banjo or "guit-tar."

A version of this ballad is frequently sung at square-dance intermissions and other social gatherings around Crossnore by Mr. Obie Johnson, one of the fine sons of Uncle Alex and himself a great friend and supporter of the school.

It goes like this, according to Mr. Obie:

> Great Granddad when the land was young
> He barred his door with the wagon tongue;
> The times was tough and the Redskins mocked,
> He said his prayers with his shotgun cocked.

Great Granddad was a busy man.
He cooked his grub in a frying pan;
He picked his teeth with a huntin' knife,
He wore the same suit all his life.

Twenty-one children came to bless
The old man's home in the wilderness;
Doubt this statement if you can,
Great Granddad was a busy man,

Twenty-one boys and not one bad,
They never got fresh with Great Granddad,
For if they had he'd 'a' been right glad
To tan their hides with a hickory gad.

He raised them rough but he raised them strong;
When their feet took hold on the road to wrong,
He straightened them out with the old ramrod,
And filled them full of the fear of God.

They grew strong in heart and hand,
A firm foundation of our land;
They made the best citizens we ever had,
We need more men like great Granddad.

Granddad died at eighty-nine,
Twenty-one boys he left behind;
Times are changed but you never can tell,
You might yet do half as well.

That old ballad, I might add, is still descriptive of the men of the mountain country as well as the wonderful old great-granddads of long-gone days. Most all of our ballads are as English as Churchill and plum pudding. And there's a good reason. The ancestors of the people in the mountains, generally speaking, came to this country from the British Isles. This fact is usually evident even to the casual visitor—for one reason, because of the speech.

For instance, many expressions in general use in the mountains today go back to Elizabethan times. They used to employ the expression "fernint" or "ferninst" a great deal when we first came here, and it is still often heard. It means opposite to or across from. Something was "over ferninst" something else. They also used the word "thronged" in a peculiar way. If one of the old folks had a particularly busy day, it was a "thronged" day. Or if a country inn was full up with people, then it was "thronged" and you had to go elsewhere.

These expressions go back to Shakespeare's times. And so, I'm of the opinion, do many of our other mountain usages and activities, such as quiltings, square dancing, bear hunting, and the like. When I first came to the mountains, quilting was one of the favorite diversions of the women and one that had its utilitarian side as well. Quiltings were held in the daytime at a woman's house. Each quilter would contribute a covered dish to the lunch. As the colorful bits of cloth were sewed into quilts, the tongues would wag, and just as colorful bits of gossip would be exchanged.

As for square dancing, I understand it's spread all over the country today and people do it even in our largest cities. Its home is in the mountains though, in a mountain cabin where a fiddler and a banjo picker and likely some lean mountain fellow with his guit-tar get to strumming and the young folks start shuffling to the cries of a caller. Two things I particularly like about square dancing—it's good exercise, and it's so democratic. Everybody dances with everybody else, rich and poor, young and old.

Neither the Doctor nor I ever had the time for bear hunting, but it's a popular sport in our mountains. Sometimes the hunters aren't out to shoot the bears but rather to capture the cubs. They can sell the cubs to circuses or keep them and use them in training their bearhounds. A dear friend of ours—a well-known lady bear hunter who doesn't want to be mentioned by name—tells an interesting story about one of those "cub hunts." It goes something like this:

"About February," she says, "the mother bears find their cubs"—that's a mountain expression for the birth of animals —"so old man Spence Shook and Lawyer John Barrier leave their dogs behind and go out a-lookin' for cubs. Pretty soon they find a den, and old man Spence crawls in. Lawyer Barrier stands guard outside, and sure enough the old bear comes back and starts in the hole. Lawyer Barrier gets a tail hold on the bear and pulls hard, but a bear's tail's not very long. Old man Spence, a-gatherin' up the cubs in the den, wants to know what's a-darkenin' the hole when suddenly Lawyer Barrier's tail hold breaks and old man Spence finds out. That bear tears the shirt right off his back and scratches him up powerful bad afore old man Spence can scramble out of that den."

That's the way she tells the story. Maybe it's more entertaining hearing about a bear hunt than it is actually going on one.

## 34

SO much for the square dancing, and ballad singing, and bear hunting. We have had gay days.

But often the clouds were dark and heavy.

In the middle thirties, for instance, I well remember the time we ran out of bread at Crossnore.

Always the bill for bread, which had to come from a bakery because we didn't have the equipment to bake our own, except biscuit, was hard to pay. On this occasion we had failed for so long to pay it that the breadman said he just could not come any more. It had been a familiar sight to see his big truck come up on the campus every other day. But now we didn't see it.

We substituted potatoes, increased the quantity of beans, made biscuits for breakfast and corn bread for supper, and did without bakery bread.

The children missed it. They wanted their bread and molasses or their bread and jelly for breakfast. And breakfast always had been a simple meal. They were unhappy.

But we kept telling them that if they would pray to God for the money with which to pay the back bill and buy the bread, and then if they would behave so well that God would think they ought to have their prayers answered, we'd get bread.

And so the month wore on, and every time they'd come to me to talk about their situation and say, "When can we get more bread?" I'd say, "Well, the best hope I can see is for the next DAR check to come in. It comes from the national office, which forwards to us all the gifts that we've been given during the month, and it'll soon be the first of the month."

We watched for the turn of that month as eagerly as we ever watched for a beautiful sunrise.

And it came.

That was the biggest check we'd had in many a day. We paid the back bill. The breadman's big truck began to come up on the campus again. We learned a lesson, and the children had been made happy.

Perhaps my recital of the arrival time after time of a large check that helped complete one phase after another of our Crossnore project may grow tiresome. I certainly do not intend for it to sound melodramatic. Nor am I trying to preach. I merely wish to testify to my belief in the power of prayer, made sincerely and in full faith to the loving Father of us all. Of course along with the prayer must go a lot of hard work.

I have recounted how the men were being educated in better farming methods by the farm agents, how the boys in agricultural classes, not only at Crossnore School but all over the county, were being made to realize the advantages of improved methods. They were readying themselves for better times. They were giving their children advantages that they had never dreamed of before. All of them, too—not just a few. And they were wanting better things for the home.

But it was the men and children that were being thus educated. The women, too, had to have something. They became concerned; they realized, for instance—and this was back in the early days of our life at Crossnore—that they shouldn't put up a hundred jars of beans—as one ambitious housewife told me tearfully that she did—and lose seventy-seven jars by having the beans spoil.

I wanted to do something about it. So I wrote that story down to Mrs. Jane McKinnon, who was then the pride of the state in home economics. She sent me from Raleigh a specialist in her department to help the women in their homes, to teach them how to can. They wanted the help, but they were bashful, they were afraid. They didn't want this specialist to see what limited kitchen equipment they had.

But I knew they had courage. A young bride who had started housekeeping—and she was destined to have great influence in Avery County—said she'd risk having the Raleigh lady come. So she invited her to her modest little home to give a demonstration. She particularly wanted the visiting lady to teach them how to can beans that wouldn't spoil.

To this housewife's great surprise the only thing the lady asked for was flour sacks—of which every mountain housekeeper had a plenty—and then she wanted to know if she had a wash boiler—and every woman did, to boil her clothes in. Next she wanted plenty of hot water. The wash boiler was put on the stove, and the hot water soon was ready.

The flour sacks were used for the blanching, and the jars were sterilized in the boiling water. The women had been

209

used to hanging the jars on sticks in the yard where the sun would shine on them; that much sterilization, they had learned, helped to make the canned things keep better.

That was a new day in Crossnore.

Other homes were opened to the visiting teacher, and one by one she visited them, and they all began to learn how to preserve their foods. Then one day the teacher said, "Why not take some lessons now in something different from canning, why not study cooking?"

The women told her, "We know how to do common cooking. What we want is for you to teach us how to make cakes and trim 'em up."

"Well, why do you want that?" she asked them.

One of them grinned bashfully. "We can win prizes at the fair if we learn how to do that," she said.

So she gave them lessons in cakemaking and cake decoration, and along with these lessons in fancy cooking she slipped in many a suggestion for better *plain* cooking. And it wasn't long until they were glad to have a home-demonstration agent in our county, and what wonderful work has been done by the women who have held that position in the years since!

In the same way we saw a quick change in the women in their interest in dressing after we began to sell secondhand clothing. These sales at Aunt Pop's and Uncle Gilmer's were offering temptations that many women of the mountains had not known before. The women could take that beautiful material that came in many of the garments and make it over to fit them—if only they knew how. So they decided that they wanted to learn to sew. They asked for sewing lessons, and we organized a sewing class.

There were so very many who came—a lady we all called affectionately by the one name "Miss Blanche" was their teacher—that they had to be divided into sections and come only two days a week. I remember one day at the beginning, a member of the class, a grandmother, said, "Miss Blanche, you won't like me for a pupil, I'm afraid, 'cause I don't hardly know which end of a needle to thread."

The patient Miss Blanche looked ever so sorry for the old lady.

But she spoke up again. "I 'spect, though, I could learn you a whole lot about a fryin' pan and a hoe handle."

Miss Blanche laughed, and the old lady's self-respect was restored.

Before that summer was over, the old lady had learned to make a pretty dress for a little girl—one of her grandchildren. And she said, "Aks Mis' Sloops to let me buy this dress and take it home. I'd rather show my old man Enoch that I had done this than to have him give me a diamond ring."

We had provided the material, but she had made the dress and it was hers, of course. She did take it home and Enoch was greatly pleased at what she had done.

So through the years we worked and we learned. I say *we* because Doctor and I were also learning; it wasn't only the native people of the mountains.

For one thing, Doctor was learning to be a psychologist. Not in the narrow professional sense, but as a man long experienced in handling people, and especially the people of our mountain region. Doctor is a wonderful physician and surgeon, and I am happy to pay tribute to his medical skill, his ability to diagnose a difficult illness, to handle his scalpel expertly. But I believe he's even better as a sort of horseback psychologist.

As an example of his proficiency in that field, I want to report the case of the old man who had the badly infected finger. And also the way he treated another patient, Aunt Marthy, wife of old Uncle Harvey. "Hairy" Harvey they called him. And I could tell about many other cases in which he used certain mountain superstitions to supplement his own treatments. Had Doctor flouted these beliefs, silly in

211

themselves of course, he not only would have offended deeply these good people, but he would have lost their confidence and very likely rendered himself useless to help them.

Doctor didn't tell me these stories—though he did confirm them when I inquired. They were first related to me by Aunt Newbie.

"I had seen this man coming up and down the road to and from the hospital," Aunt Newbie said, "and I saw that he had a big bandage on one finger. Then one day I went over to the hospital to get the nurse, Mrs. Stevenson, and take her out riding. I thought that she needed some recreation, because she had been staying so closely on the job.

" 'You need to have more fun than you do,' I said to her," said Aunt Newbie. " 'You don't get out enough.'

" 'Well,' she said, 'I don't get out much, but I have a lot of fun with my flowers, and working them takes a good deal of my time. And then, too, Dr. Sloop is the funniest man.' And her face brightened up—she didn't laugh a lot, but she laughed all over her face—and she said, 'Now, for example, this morning, this man has been coming to the hospital with a finger that's almost rotted off'—those are the words she used—'it's so badly infected.'

" 'But now the finger's gotten well to the point that Dr. Sloop dresses it one day and the man at his home dresses it the next day, and that saves Dr. Sloop's time. Well, this morning, Dr. Sloop was warning him about destroying those bandages so that the infection wouldn't get to some other place on his skin or infect other people.'

" 'Dr. Sloop said not to let the discarded bandage touch anything, but just drop it in the fire. But the man was distressed and he said, "Oh, Doc, but I've always heared that no sore would heal up if'n you burnt the rag that was around it."

"And Dr. Sloop said, 'Oh, that's only if you watch it burn.

You shouldn't watch the bandage burn, and then it will be all right.'"

So the man went away happy. His belief hadn't been disturbed, and yet he was going to do what Doctor had told him to do.

Aunt Newbie said she heard too that Aunt Marthy had expressed alarm at the prospect of burning an infected bandage and Doctor told her there'd be no danger if she stood in front of the fireplace with her back to it and threw the bandage over her left shoulder into the fire and then walked away without looking back as the bandage burned.

And Aunt Marthy had happily followed his instructions. Further infections had been prevented, and she had joyfully held to her faith in hexing.

But Doctor has been learning things in other fields, too, in the more than twoscore years we have been living in the mountains. He is a great one for hobbies. But I'll tell about only one of them.

Doctor's a weatherman.

He's what the United States Weather Bureau describes as a "cooperative observer." I suppose that means mainly that he's a free observer; he doesn't get pay for his recording and reporting. However he gets a tremendous amount of fun and satisfaction out of keeping up with our Crossnore weather.

Doctor has been making daily weather observations since 1908, and he's been listed as a cooperative observer since 1938. He takes his readings at noon and at midnight each day; if he's away from home, he sees to it that our son Will or someone else takes those precious readings. We've got weather instruments on our roof—which is flat and made of concrete—in the living room, and in the backyard. At noon Doctor takes the temperature reading and the barometric pressure and these he carefully records, and at midnight he records the maximum and minimum temperature readings for the day and also puts down the amount of rainfall, snowfall, or sleet or hail. Then he makes up a report at the end of the month, a day-by-day recording, which he sends to the weather bureau. He sends to the Tennessee Valley Authority, the *Tri-County News* at Spruce Pine, and the *Avery County News* at Newland copies of this report. It's a lot of work, but Doctor enjoys doing it, and it is a valuable service.

Now he uses standard weather-recording instruments, but when he started off, he used a thermometer he had made himself. He took a glass tube, blew mercury into it, sealed it, and then marked calibrations on it to provide a temperature scale. It was quite a task, but then Doctor was always eager to accomplish something challenging.

I have had little to do with this weather-recording hobby, but I did ask him one day what was the highest temperature recording and also the lowest. He told me that the highest was $91°F$. in 1926 and the lowest was $-15°F$., recorded in 1917. He also told me that in following his habit of comparing our Crossnore climate with that of Asheville he had learned that Crossnore's weather averages three or four degrees below Asheville. But it should, for we are some 1300 feet higher.

## 35

IN 1947, if I recall correctly, we were visited by a state inspector. I'll never forget that visit.

We always said that everything we did at Crossnore must be up to standard. I sought to impress upon the children, the teachers, and everybody on our staff the importance of doing things right, of maintaining high standards in everything we undertook. We had our high school standardized almost from the start. Our business department that was added some time later was subject, too, to regular inspection by state authorities.

So we were not surprised when the welfare department of North Carolina, which does such a thorough job, sent an inspector to Crossnore to see if our dormitories were being kept up to snuff. We weren't surprised, but we were a little concerned, for I had been conscious of the fact that for some time our Big Boys' dormitory was worse than a barn.

We had tried and tried to get money with which to build a new one, but this time we hadn't been successful. Whenever we had been able to raise a small fund for that purpose, we'd find some other more pressing need. So I dreaded the inspector's going up on the hill to visit that dormitory. I was afraid she would condemn it and never let us open it again as a dormitory.

Some time before, I had gone over there and had found the doors in terrible condition. The boys had put locks on them and they'd lose their keys, and then they'd cut chunks out of the doors to get them open. I hadn't realized it was happening. As I examined those doors I found that most of them were in very poor condition. I decided they could just do without doors in that dormitory, so I had the doors taken down. I told them, "Now we're going to learn not to mutilate a building just because we lose a key, or else we'll not be allowed to stay in our new dormitory which I know we're going to get some day."

A terrible howl went up, but soon they grew accustomed to having curtains hanging where the doors had been. That had happened before the inspector came.

So after going around to all the dormitories, the inspector came back to me and said that this was wrong and that was wrong, that there were too many children in the dormitories, that they were crowded into too small space. And she proceeded to tell me how many cubic feet to every occupant there must be in every sleeping room. She said she felt that we

215

should send half the children home until we could build more dormitories.

I said, "You know the thing I was afraid you'd do when you went out there was to tell me I couldn't use that Big Boys' dormitory any more, because it is crowded and it is bad and I'm ashamed of it."

"Well," she said with a smile, "to tell you the truth, it is worse than any of the others, but we can't condemn it, because it is warm and it can be cleaned, and the trouble is that we can't measure the cubic feet of air space in each room, because there are no doors to it and there's no way of measuring how much air comes into the room from outside."

"You know, you've given me a wonderful idea," I said. "Now I'll not have to send half the children from the other dormitories home. I'll just take down all the doors from the bedrooms. And that solves still another problem. We have just bought a truckload of stuff from the War Assets Administration and had to borrow the money to pay for it. I can sell those doors for enough to pay off that note at the bank. I'm just as thankful to you as I can be, and I hope you'll come again."

And that's just what I did! I'm not joking. I had the doors to the rooms removed, and I sold them. They brought good money, too.

There are no inside doors to the rooms in our new dormitories. We use nothing but curtains. Our dormitories are constructed in the interior on what you might describe as a barracks plan. And the no-doors policy lets us conserve heat in wintertime and gives us more effective ventilation. Besides, without doors, housemothers and housefathers can keep a better watch on their charges.

It works wonderfully well. I am really delighted at the good fortune that brought that state inspector to Crossnore.

# 36

THAT business about the doors will serve to illustrate how it has been at Crossnore all through the years. We've found that if one thing seems to get you down, something shortly happens to get you up again.

And now, like any talkative doting mother, I want to tell you about our children—not Crossnore's thousands but the Doctor's and my two. They are highly useful citizens in our own community, and nothing can please any parents more than to be able to say that. Emma went off to college at Mount Holyoke, took her last two years at Duke and then attended the medical school of Vanderbilt University. She is now in charge of our hospital during the daytime, and if I do say it, Emma's a wonderful doctor. And she's one busy soul, for although Crossnore has less than 300 population within the town limits, patients come from miles around.

Will went to the University of North Carolina and then took his work in dentistry at Atlanta Southern. He's another busy one. Emma has three children, two girls and a boy. Will has two boys. The five children's parents contend—unreasonably, of course—that Doctor and I spoil them. But even if we did, I'd maintain that we had a right to. We're all human, especially grandparents.

And now I want to tell you of something else, and I hope my vanity will be pardoned. Anyway, it's a part of the Crossnore story.

One day Emma reminded me that the North Carolina Federation of Women's Clubs was soon to have its convention in Charlotte. She said she wanted me to make plans to go.

I told her I didn't think I could.

"Now, Mother, you must," said Emma. "I insist that you go. You'll have a good time." But she saw that she wasn't making much of an impression. She grinned. "You know, they're announcing the North Carolina Mother of the Year at that meeting, and if you're named you'll certainly have to be there to get the award."

"Oh, pshaw!" I said. "I've no idea I'll be the one."

"But you must go anyway. You'll enjoy it, and you need to get away for a few days." Emma was determined.

I knew that some of the ladies had been working on a project to get me selected as the North Carolina Mother of the Year. But I hadn't heard what had come of the project.

The time of the meeting came on, and I did go. Then came the night of the banquet. Senator Clyde Hoey, who had been governor, one of my very good friends, came down from Washington to make the address. He made a fine one, too. And toward the close he said he had been asked to announce the committee's selection for the annual Mother of the Year award.

He said a few more words—enough to build the situation into one properly dramatic, as he can always do so effectively —and then he made the announcement.

I was it.

The committee's decision that I should be so honored pleased me immensely, and I was grateful as I went back to Crossnore. But I certainly did not think it would go any further than that. I was not prepared for a telephone message I received some time later.

Doctor and I were in Asheville, at the S & W Cafeteria, to be exact. We had gone there on our weekly trip to have dinner and then see a movie. While we were eating a gentleman came up to our table and told me that I was wanted on the telephone and that the person calling seemed most eager to talk with me immediately. So I went.

"Is this Dr. Mary Martin Sloop?" the young man asked. I could tell he was young by his voice.

"Yes, it is," I said.

He told me that he was a reporter on the staff of the *Asheville Citizen*, the morning newspaper there. They had just received a dispatch, he said, and they were very anxious to get a story and a picture.

"Of me?" I asked, incredulous.

"Yes, Dr. Sloop," said the young man. "I have wonderful news for you. It has just been announced that you have been selected Mother of the Year. I want to congratulate you."

But that was all weeks ago. Why was he bothering me now? "I know that. I was at the meeting of the State Federation of Women's Clubs in Charlotte when it was announced, and Senator Hoey made a speech at the banquet. But thank you anyway."

"No, Dr. Sloop, you don't understand. You have been selected *the American* Mother of the Year."

Well, I was flabbergasted. When I had recovered a bit, I told the young man he could come around to the cafeteria, and I went back to the table.

"I'm in for trouble," I told Doctor, as I sat down.

He looked at me, a bit puzzled. But he wasn't alarmed. "What have you done now?" he asked.

"That was a reporter for the *Citizen* who called me. He wanted to come over and bring a photographer to get a story and picture."

"Of you?"

"Yes. He told me that I had been selected the American Mother of the Year."

Doctor just looked at me, and a big grin spread over his face. "Humph!" That's all he said.

Everybody loves being made a fuss of and I am no exception. That trip to New York was a barrel of fun, from beginning to end. My husband, the one who deserves the most credit for Crossnore's development, had to stay home to tend the hospital, but my daughter Emma came along to see that

I behaved myself. At the station to meet us were troops of Boy Scouts, scores of photographers, and a delegation of ladies from the Golden Rule Foundation which sponsors the selection. Someone shoved a bunch of red roses into my arms while someone else "welcomed" me to New York. I felt like an antique movie star.

I hadn't been to New York in fifteen years and everything seemed big, busy, and noisy. When they told us we were to stay at the Waldorf I said to Emma, "Good, I've always wanted to meet General MacArthur and President Hoover and that's where they live. I'll probably meet them someday in the elevator."

Emma laughed. "General MacArthur and President Hoover have apartments in the Towers, Mother. You'll never see them."

Every time I got into the elevator I looked for them, but Emma was right. The Waldorf is a big place and I never set eyes on either of those fine gentlemen.

Our suite at the hotel seemed as large as the lobby downstairs and just as full of people most the time—photographers, girl reporters, a lady who wanted to paint my picture, a man who wanted to give me a cookbook, three people who wanted to give me a lamp. The lamp, one of them said, was a representation of an antique and it sold for one hundred dollars.

"That's lovely," I said, "but what'll I do with it?" I was thinking of my five rough-and-tumble grandchildren and my little mountain house.

One of the men eyed me peculiarly. "Why of course you'll put it in your home."

I did appreciate their kindness. I took that lamp home and gave it to a neighbor who has no children. She put it back in a corner and placed some furniture in front of it for protection. You can't see it very well, but it's there.

I must tell you about having my picture painted. My second morning in New York I was talking with five ladies from the

220

press when a quiet little lady came up and said, "Mrs. Sloop, I'm sorry but I have waited just as long as I can. Now you must come with me."

She had, it seems, painted the portrait of every American Mother of the Year so far and she wasn't going to stop now. I thought of the hours, the days you have to sit for your portrait, and I objected violently. But she reassured me. "Don't worry. This portrait has to be finished right away. It goes on exhibit in Newark tomorrow."

She had in her hand a bunch of paint brushes that varied from the tiniest little thread to one about four inches wide. I pointed to it and said, "Why that's the kind we use for putting on whitewash down home."

She didn't think that was much of a joke. So I just sat quietly and in a minute or two went sound asleep, my head on my chest. When I waked up there wasn't a soul in the room but the two of us. I apologized for falling asleep but she answered, "Why you were perfectly splendid. You didn't move a muscle the whole time you were asleep." I was going to ask her how she got my face with my head on my chest but I decided not to.

I looked at the portrait and it wasn't anybody I'd ever seen before. She asked me if I wanted anything changed. "Changed?" I answered. "Oh I wouldn't have you change anything for the world." Then I was a free bird, and the little lady took my portrait off to New Jersey. Maybe the people of Newark liked it.

There were so many nice luncheons and dinners and receptions that I can't remember them all. At one a very lovely blond lady in a clever little hat and stunning clothes came up to me and asked, "Are you Mrs. Sloop?"

"Yes, I am."

"I'm Mrs. Impellitteri," she said.

I answered that I was so happy to meet her and we chatted a moment. She was very nice. When she turned away to speak with someone else, I nudged the lady beside me. "Who's Mrs. Impellitteri?"

The lady seemed deeply shocked. "Why, she's the wife of the mayor of New York!"

I felt bad about not knowing. But then, the mayor of Crossnore is Jeeter Vance, and there probably aren't many New Yorkers who know that.

I shall never forget the luncheon at which they presented me with the award. The room was very crowded, and as our party filed between the rows of standing guests toward the speakers' table I heard a little group start singing "Ho for Carolina!" It was thrilling; I felt almost back home. I remembered Doctor then, back at the hospital. I remembered all the others who had put so much of themselves into Crossnore. I knew that this award wasn't for me at all. It was for my people of the mountains.

Eventually that wonderful trip came to an end and we returned home.

A short time afterward I went to see my sister in Davidson. I was wearing the hat and suit I had worn in New York, and my niece Lucy complimented me on it.

"Gee, Aunt Mary, you look so nice, real stylish-looking. You must have bought that outfit in New York."

I laughed until the tears came. It's wonderful how people's minds work. I'd been wearing the hat for two years and it was second hand when the lady gave it to me. I'd already worn out two sets of feathers on it. As for the suit, I'd bought it, and probably third hand, at Aunt Pop's and Uncle Gilmer's Store.

But New York didn't object. I got along fine.

# 37

ONCE back in Crossnore, I was anxious to get on with my work. A young friend of fifty shook her head, amazed. "I just can't understand it," she said. "You get up early, fix your own breakfast, get down to the school office by eight, go like a house afire all day, make a speech in the evening, and square dance the rest of the night."

Like nearly all flattering speeches, this is an exaggeration. I usually quit square dancing by eleven. But I have always thanked the Lord for my durable physique and am duly appreciative that He has kept me on my feet these eighty years.

But recently I was ill, so ill that my daughter Emma put me in the hospital and talked mighty straight to me. She gave orders and I listened meekly. Of course she had me flat on my back.

I was allowed only a few visitors and so I had plenty of time to think. One of the things I enjoyed most was reviewing our medical work here in Linville Valley. Although a good deal of my efforts have been in the educational field, I guess I'm still a doctor at heart.

When we first came to the mountains, old superstitions were strong and faith in modern science was weak. Sanitation, as we know it today, was unknown, and preventive medicine was just plain foolishness. I had many a one say to me in the old days, "I ain't no fool and you can't tell me that stickin' a hole in a young'un with a needle can cure diphtheria or keep off typhoid fever."

"Givin' in" to sickness was considered a weakness and endurance was rigidly cultivated. Many were mighty slow to send for a doctor. When finally they did, they'd expect us to cure a case of double pneumonia in one visit. And that was long before the days of penicillin!

What seem like simple things to us now—for instance, that people with contagious diseases shouldn't have visitors—were hard to get across a few years back. Turning kindly people away who had come to "sit up" with the sick one seemed so inhospitable. As a result, diseases like diphtheria were common, and usually in epidemic proportions. The Doctor and I held front-porch clinics to administer preventative shots, but very few came and we were discouraged at first. Ultimately, the basic open-mindedness of the mountain people allowed us to win them over to our side.

In the same way people are losing their fear of the hospital, and it's easy to see why. In the old days, it was a difficult and even dangerous task to bring a sick person to the hospital. It meant a long ride in a springless wagon over a rough road, and usually the patient was very sick indeed before his relatives would even consider the trip. Because the patient often died on the way, or shortly afterward, people would say, "Most folks you take to the hospital just die." Nowadays good roads and modern automobiles have helped change all that. Even ambulances aren't too expensive.

Small hospitals like ours are usually "mighty nigh full," as the folks say. In the mountains, where large families are such a source of pride, the mothers and babies form a large proportion of our patients, I'm glad to say. The babies arrive in singles most of the time, but once we had triplets and I'll never forget it. They weighed but 10 pounds, the three of them, and we sorely needed an incubator. But they got along all right without one and now, ten years later, they are back at Crossnore as boarding pupils.

I recall two heart-warming incidents in connection with the birth of those triplets. When the news of their arrival spread through the valley, the Carnation Milk Company, which has a receiving depot for raw milk some fifteen miles from Crossnore, sent a man up to tell us that they would like to furnish milk for the three babies free of charge for the first year. Now I call that right friendly.

The triplets remained in the hospital for a whole year, and then their proud father came to take them home. Before he left, he reached into his pocket and solemnly brought forth a fifty-cent piece which he gave us as payment for his bill.

Sometimes the folks won't let even my daughter Emma treat them but insist on "the old Doctor." That's my husband, of course. He goes on duty late in the afternoon and often there's a throng waiting for him. If he can't get to them right away, they just keep on waiting for him. It's a sight to see, if you walk into that waiting room about midnight, and the crowd is still there.

There's still another member of the Sloop doctoring clan besides Doctor, Emma, Will, and myself, and I want to tell about him. Not so many years ago Doctor's nephew, his sister's child, used to visit us as a boy. Eustace Henry Smith was named for my husband and always called him "Uncle Doctor."

"When I get grown," he used to tell us, "I'm going to be a doctor and live in Crossnore and help Uncle Doctor." Now, a lot of water goes under the bridge before a boy "gets grown," and I don't know that we took Eustace too seriously. But that's exactly what he did. He went off to medical school, came back with his M.D., and hung out his shingle in Crossnore. Today Eustace is a fine physician with a steadily growing practice and he certainly is a help to Uncle Doctor. . . .

These are some of the thoughts I had in the hospital when they finally made this old doctor a patient. We've come a long way since I used to assist Doctor in those open-air operations under the apple tree.

# 38

MORE than a year has passed since my exciting trip to New York. Now we have a new American Mother of the Year, a Chinese woman of California who certainly must deserve all the fine tributes that have been paid her. I have not met her, for I was unable to attend the meeting in New York at which the award was officially presented. That came during the time that I was in the hospital.

My year as Mother came between an Indian mother and a Chinese mother. Some years ago a Negro woman was Mother. I think all this testifies to the greatness of America, to the goodness of heart of the people of this wonderful nation, to the fact that we are truly a democracy. I am happy to have been numbered among these women. It has been a rewarding experience, and I am deeply grateful. I had to make quite a number of speeches because of my office, but I didn't mind that. In fact, I suspect I enjoyed it. I was always ready to make a speech—about Crossnore—at the drop of a hat. I plan to make many more—about Crossnore.

Crossnore, after all, is my enthusiasm—my third child, my other self. I delight to make speeches about the school. I have enjoyed telling the Crossnore story.

The story is about ended—my telling of it. I sit here in my office and look down the hill to the little circular flat where the story began. I turn and look out through the doorway at the left up the hill until the hill lifts out of my line of vision. I hope that will be the way the story of Crossnore continues. I am glad I can see no ending to that story.

Perhaps I have been haphazard in telling it. I have jumped about a bit, and have failed at times to keep the chronology straight. Always in telling one story I am quickly reminded of another, and frequently the first story may have happened many years before or after the second. So I get my periods mixed. But it matters little, I believe. Taken together, bunched in one, they make the story of Crossnore.

I can hear right now the ringing of hammers, and the insistent steady whine of an electric saw. Construction. Progress. Building for Crossnore. More opportunity for the children—the bright, ambitious, sturdy American children of our mountains! There can be no sweeter music to my old ears.

I look toward the source of the welcome sound. I cannot see the work under construction, but I can see many other buildings. These are my joy, these are my other children. As they say it in the mountains, I feel almost as though I had *birthed* each one of them. Some of them I have mentioned; others I have spoken of in detail. Perhaps some I have overlooked. I'll call the roll, for though I cannot see them all as I look up the hill, I can see each stone and piece of timber in my mind's eye: Big Boys', Middle Boys', Old Big Boys' (now being made into our new laundry), Old Print Shop, the infirmary, the gymnasium, Little Boys', Little Girls', Big Girls', music building, dining hall and kitchen, Old Middle Girls', New Middle Girls', the bell tower, the lunchroom (at the new high school), the sewing building, the weaving building, the old laundry, Aunt Pop's and Uncle Gilmer's Sales Store, and the Administration Building, where I now sit, all of them the property of Crossnore, Inc.; and five others, the property of Avery County but contributing to our progam just as though they were our own: the old gymnasium, the agricultural shop, the old primary building, the old grammar-grades building, and the present handsome Crossnore high-school building.

But, as much as we appreciate them, the buildings themselves—stone, brick, concrete, timber—are not of primary importance. It's what they stand for that counts: a chance at a fine new life for countless children.

No one else is about my office at the moment. I can hear the children playing up on the hill; I can look out the window and see four girls in their plaid blouses and blue jeans tripping down the road that leads to the village; in the apartment above I can hear one of the teachers stirring about, cleaning her room, perhaps. But for this one moment—and how few they are!—I am alone. For this one moment I have no problem related to the school to consider and no decisions to make. The next moment the telephone may ring and a mother in Johnson City, Tennessee, or Boone or North Wilkesboro may ask me to see that her little Johnny gets the right sort of shoes with the money she is sending me, or somebody may be inviting me off to make a speech, or Mrs. William Henry Belk, or Mrs. Preston B. Wilkes, Jr., of Charlotte, or Mrs. John S. Welborn of High Point, or Miss Virginia Horne of Wadesboro, all of them DARs and all members of our Crossnore board of trustees—and what friends of Crossnore they are—may be suggesting some action to take at the next board meeting. Anything may happen in the next moment, but just now I am alone. Perhaps this is the time to speak of my philosophy of life.

Once in a while somebody asks me to reveal it.

I'm not sure that I know what that means. I do know that my eighty years of living—I'll be eighty on March 9, 1953— have enabled me to say that I firmly believe that Christian education is the cure for all the ills of this sick world. I'm grateful that my early home was on the campus of a church-affiliated college, that I was graduated from a junior college under the care of the church, and that I could incorporate into the first charter of Crossnore, Inc., the statement that the corporation was formed for the "promotion of Christian education."

I have been in this world a long time; I go well back into the days of Queen Victoria. Perhaps in some ways I am indeed Victorian, and I might be expected to be Victorian in my ideas of discipline, particularly in the school. Yet I have always held that corporal punishment in any institution is a mistake and fails to produce the results wanted in a vast majority of cases. Perhaps this is largely due to the fact that it is hard to get together a number of persons in authority

228

who are really wise in administering such punishment, but I still believe that it is unwise—even in families.

I am happy to say that I have lived to see that theory grow in favor all over the United States, even in our penal institutions. And surely the stories we have read and heard of conditions in war prisons have made us realize in more graphic manner the horror of it.

Cultivating one's conscience is another favorite doctrine of mine, and we try to teach it to our students through the motto we have always had for our campus, "Noblesse Oblige," the need for educating ourselves to be prompted to do right by the nobility in our hearts, and that to do this we must each night look back on the day and see if we have kept our conduct in line with all of the Ten Commandments, upon which are based the teachings of Christ.

I believe that prayer is tremendously important in life. I believe that God not only gives us moral strength to do right and resist wrong, but also that He gives us the ability to think and to act when we are in need. I believe that He expects us to use all the talent and strength we have to help ourselves or to think our way out of a difficulty, but that when we have done all we can, we tell Him so and ask Him to make possible what seems to us impossible. Then we see the way open up. This I know, to the utter truth of this I can testify.

And God always expects our thanks for what He does for us, not only thanks in words but in conduct. We must show our appreciation and let the world know that we believe in the power of prayer. And we must remember that our conduct has much to do with the answer to our prayers. It is the righteous whose prayers prevail.

Beyond the coves and the ridges and the impenetrable thick forests, yonder towers old Grandfather. I cannot see him at the moment because a shifting cloud envelops him. But I *know* he is there. Presently the cloud will be gone and out of ancient, kindly eyes Grandfather will be smiling down upon me. Even more surely I know that God *is*, and that He will show His smiling face if I, through prayer and faith, remove the cloud that may be separating us.

Crossnore is the product of many things—the inherent strength and nobility of the mountain people whom it serves, the generosity of the DAR women and the churches and the countless other good people who have through the years given it their support, the love and care of the boys and girls who have helped to nourish it. But far and beyond all else, Crossnore is the product of prayer. Prayer has wrought miracles in these hills. I know it. Through long years I have seen it. Joyously and out of a full heart I declare it. If any would doubt the power of prayer, only this I say to him, and humbly: Try it.

You ask me, then, what is my philosophy. I am at last—and how strange that is and how I hate to admit it—at a loss for words. I have had a long life, a full life, a happy life. In some respects, I have had an achieving life, though I haven't done as much as I hoped to do—and I'm not stopping yet either. I have had a devoted partner through these long years, and I wish to pay tribute to him. You know, folks occasionally say to me, "Mrs. Sloop, you're so smart; you get so much done; you must have a lot of brains." Well, I want to tell you that the greater part of whatever success I have achieved is due to Doctor. He's the quiet kind, but he's got twice as much sense as I have—I'm mostly mouth. He should have the credit for a lot of things I get credit for doing. But Doctor would not want it that way. He'd rather stay in the back of the hall and let me take the bows from the stage. But always I've known he was there.

Work and pray. Maybe that's my philosophy. I have always been busy. I have worked hard, but I have enjoyed it. One of the finest compliments I ever had was from a friend who visited us here. After watching me for a day or two he said to me: "Mrs. Sloop, my father used to speak of a certain man he knew, a man who was full of energy and always doing things, as 'a steam engine in britches.' Well, I'll have to say that you're 'a steam engine in skirts.'"

I laughed. "Maybe it'd be more descriptive to call me 'a steam engine in old clothes,'" I told him.

But what he said pleased me very much. I wouldn't want anybody to think I was lazy. I don't see how anybody would want to go through life without working—and working hard.

Nor do I see how anybody could be ingrate enough to spend his life without praying—and praying often. And how could a lazy, trifling fellow have enough brass to ask the Lord for anything?

Work and pray. Yes, and have faith. Not a puny faith that any ill wind might blow away. Seek to emulate the utter and complete faith of the young and beautiful Nazarene. Jesus spoke always of God as the Father. We should know Him too as the loving and all-wise and all-powerful Father. And we should never hesitate to ask Him to help us. He will. Faith is the very cornerstone of Crossnore.

Perhaps now I have revealed my philosophy. I have never taken time to try to figure it out. I have always been too busy. I am still that way. There are other buildings we are planning for Crossnore. With materials restricted, it's going to take a lot of maneuvering. The new recreation building, for instance. That is needed badly. And new furniture, and better living quarters for many of the faculty people. Down in the village, too, there's much to be done. Nor have I mentioned the need of a new supervising housekeeper, or homemaker, who will not live in any one dormitory but will inspect, oversee, and advise about each and every building on the campus. This will require a person with training and tact, one who can deliver the goods. And speeches! Oh my, the DAR meetings, the Lions clubs, and the other groups I'll be called on to address! And I'll love it! And now, of all things, .writing a book!

So—where was I? Oh, yes, my philosophy.

Perhaps it's work and pray and have faith. And then, don't worry. I'm not worrying. I'm not worrying about what's going to happen to Crossnore when I'm gone. I'm only just a little envious of the one who's going to have such a fine time helping so many marvelous things happen here.

I know things will be all right—for Crossnore and for me. For Crossnore I cherish—and see—a long and even more accomplishing life, a continually increasing importance to the youth of our beloved mountains. For me the calendar says —the calendar, mind you, and not I—that I must now be entering the uncharted maze of days along the highest slope of the last mountain. And below it there'll be the shadows of the farthest cove. But little that matters. Beyond the cove—and this I know—I shall shortly walk out into the unending Sunshine.

There, I trust, I shall quickly find work to do.

CPSIA information can be obtained
at www.ICGtesting.com
Printed in the USA
LVOW10s0502230217
525146LV00006BA/505/P